A Concise Guide to Music Theory

PERRY GOLDSTEIN

STONY BROOK UNIVERSITY

KENDALL/HUNT PUBLISHING COMPANY
4050 Westmark Drive   Dubuque, Iowa 52002

Cover artwork by Benjye Troob, www.benjye.com.

Contents

Introduction

Rudiments of Music: A Concise Guide to Music Theory is written for the beginner who has an interest in reading and writing music as well as the desire to understand the rudiments of tonal music theory. It will also be useful for the student who has experience of music notation and the desire for a stronger foundation in the rudiments of music. This book covers basic notation of pitch and rhythm, major and minor keys, intervals, triads, and the tonal context of harmony. Students will also learn how to compose short rhythm examples, melodies in major and minor keys, and a 24-measure piece for piano, exploring the principles of melody and harmony. This book is intended to supplement the classroom experience. The study of music theory requires two basic components: the study of theory and the application of theory through the listening experience. This book supplies the former, the basics of music theory. The application of theory through listening will be provided in the classroom. It is the hope of the author that the merely theoretical will be brought to life in the experience of music, and for this the work of the instructor in a beginning theory class is crucial. Understanding how chords, intervals, meters, key signatures, and melodies work can only be meaningful when they explicate the listening, performing, and composing experience of music. The study of theory is a desiccated endeavor when it does not answer questions about how we listen to, and experience, music.

I have over a dozen years of experience teaching non-majors at Stony Brook University to thank for the impetus to write this book, which attempts to teach the essentials of theory in a systematic way. After completing this rudimentary course in theory, the student will be ready to move on to a course in tonal harmony such as those typically taught to college freshmen in music programs. This book will supply students with all the fundamentals necessary to begin such a course with confidence. In addition, the knowledge gained through this book will provide students with the foundation necessary to go on to more advanced courses for non-majors in music history, theory, and musicianship. Students wishing to improve their skills in musicianship (sight-singing and ear-training) are encouraged to take a rudimentary course in the subject simultaneously or after finishing a course in fundamental theory.

This book would not have been possible, nor would I have desired to write it, without the dozens of teaching assistants who have taught the Elements of Music course at Stony Brook University under my supervision. It is my hope that this book will make the teaching of the course easier for them, just as their boundless enthusiasm and energy in teaching the course has made the writing of this book easier for me.

I would also like to thank my editors at Kendall/Hunt, Billee Jo Heffel and Kimberly Terry, and acquisitions editor Sue Saad for making the production of this book such a pleasant experience. I appreciate the willingness of Kendall/Hunt to make this book available to students at a reasonable cost. I am also grateful for the cheerful help of Joseph Bartolozzi in preparing this manuscript.

Last, but certainly not least, I would like to thank my wife, Dawn, for her enduring patience and support for this and so many other projects.

Pitch

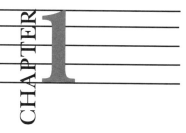

Pitch and rhythm are two of the most important elements of Western music. The scientific term for pitch is "frequency," indicating the speed at which the object making the sound—string, reed, larynx, etc.—is vibrating. The slower the vibration, the lower the sound; conversely, the faster the vibration, the higher the sound. The human ear can perceive a wide range of sounds, from very low to very high, and instruments have been created to take advantage of that capacity.

Most systems of Western music only make use of twelve distinct pitches. Although there are eighty-eight keys on the piano, for example, there are only twelve different actual pitches, and this set of twelve pitches is reproduced at various levels from low to high along the spectrum of possible sounds on the piano. Looking at a replica of the keyboard, represented below, you will see seven complete sets of twelve notes. As you look from left to right, you will see that each set contains twelve notes and is duplicated exactly as your eyes travel "up" the keyboard, which is arranged from lowest to highest notes.

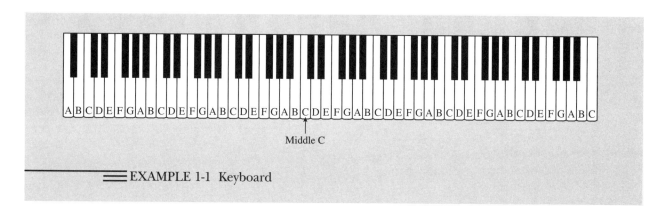

Middle C

EXAMPLE 1-1 Keyboard

Fortunately for the student of music, the system designed to describe pitch in Western music is a simple one, based on the Latin alphabet. There are only seven note names, the first seven letters of the alphabet:

a   b   c   d   e   f   g

These letters correspond to the seven white notes on the keyboard. To name the remaining five notes, the letters have **accidentals** added to them. Before treating these accidentals, however, it is necessary to describe how pitches are notated.

CLEFS

Just as the system of using the first seven letters of the Latin alphabet as the basis for describing pitches is simple, the method for notating pitch is also straightforward. Five lines, called a **staff** (plural **staves**), and lines added above or below the staff, called **ledger lines,** suffice to represent most of the notes from very low to very high. The way this is accomplished so compactly is through the use of **clefs,** which are symbols, on the far left side of the staff, that tell the player or singer in what part of the sound spectrum—low, middle, or high—to play or sing. While notes from the various clefs overlap, the different clefs "specialize." The **treble clef** is effective for higher sounding instruments or voices. The two most commonly used **C clefs** are useful for middle register music. The **bass** clef is ideal for the representation of low sounds.

Treble or "G" Clef

The mid- to upper-register **treble clef** is also called the **G clef,** because the curlicue at the bottom right of the clef surrounds the note "g," specifically middle "g." Looking at the keyboard below, you'll notice that "g" is on the second line from the bottom. Using the alphabet, we always count from "a" to "g," then return to "a" and start the process over again. Note the names of the pitches and where they lie on the staff. The treble clef is used for many instruments including flute, oboe, clarinet, trumpet, French horn, violin, among others. Tenor, alto, and soprano voice also read the treble clef.

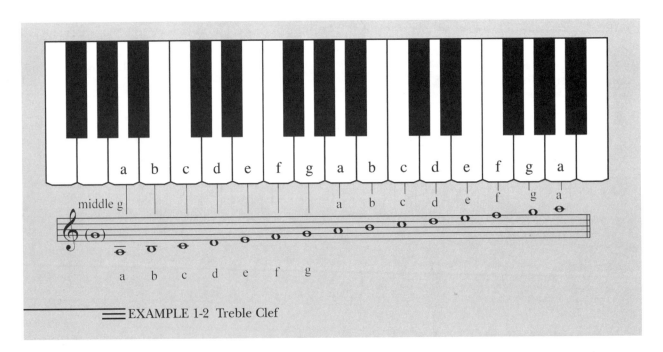

EXAMPLE 1-2 Treble Clef

Bass or "F" Clef

The low- to mid-register **bass clef** is also called the **F clef,** because the two dots at the upper right corner of the clef indicate the note "f," specifically the "f" below middle "c." Notice on the keyboard in Example 1-3 where "f" is. Once again, the sequence of notes is the first seven letters of the alphabet. Instruments with deeper sounds use this clef, including bassoon, bass clarinet, tuba, trombone, stringed bass, cello, among others. The bass clef is also used to notate the bass singing voice.

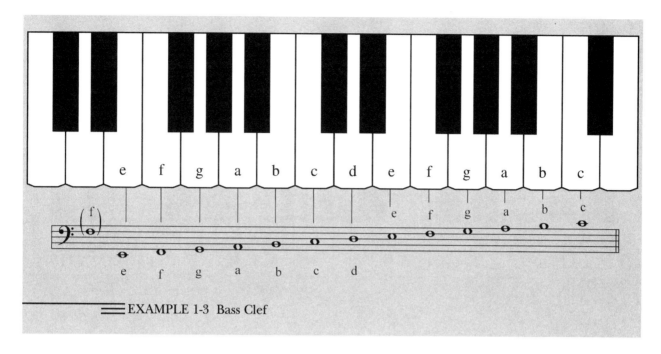

EXAMPLE 1-3 Bass Clef

"C" Clef

Unlike the treble and bass clefs, which are always found in their same positions on the staff, the "c" clef moves to different lines to represent the note middle "c." In past times, the "c" clef could be found on any line of the staff. In more recent times, the clef is used in two positions, on the third line from the top of the staff, and on the second line from the top of the staff.

"C" Alto Clef

When placed on the middle line of the staff (third from top or bottom), the "c" clef is called the **alto clef.** This is the predominant clef of the viola. Note that the prongs on top and bottom of the clef clear a space for and thus indicate the note "c."

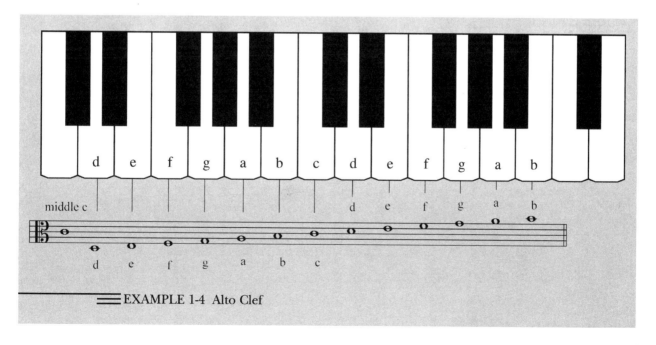

EXAMPLE 1-4 Alto Clef

"C" Tenor Clef

When placed on the second line from the top of the staff, the "c" clef is called the **tenor clef.** This clef is used to indicate higher notes on the bassoon, cello, and trombone. Once again, the prongs on top and bottom of the clef clear a space for "c."

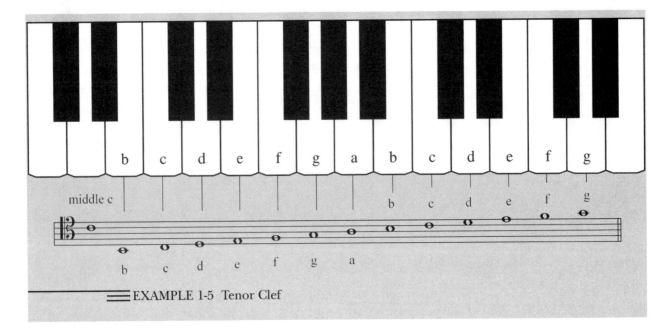

EXAMPLE 1-5 Tenor Clef

Grand Staff

The **grand staff** combines the bass and treble clefs in one unit to create a continuum from low to high notes. The grand staff is useful for instruments with a wide range, such as the piano, harp, and marimba. Note that the top line of the bass clef and the bottom line of the treble clef represent the same note—middle "c." Through the use of ledger lines, there can be considerable overlap between the higher notes of the bass clef and the lower notes of the treble clef.

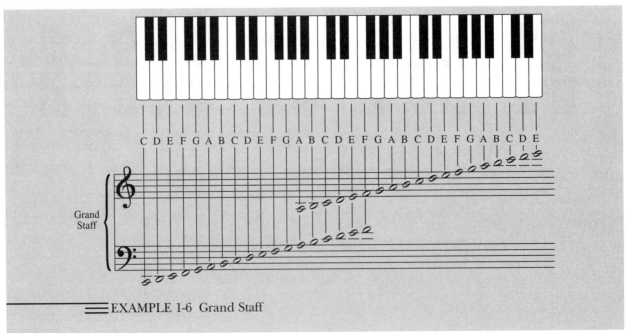

EXAMPLE 1-6 Grand Staff

Ledger Lines

Ledger lines are lines added above or below a staff to extend the notes it can represent. Any clef may add ledger lines; typically, composers try to limit the number of ledger lines to three. You'll notice in the example below that the ledger lines in either direction simply continue the sequence of notes from a through g.

G A B C D E F G A B C D E F G A B C D

EXAMPLE 1-7 Ledger Lines

The Octave Sign

A musician reading any piece of music has a great deal of information to take in and has little time to so. There are many abbreviations and symbols in music to make the musician's task simpler. Reading many ledger lines is cumbersome for musicians, so composers try to avoid writing too many. When music goes lower or higher than is comfortable, a composer will use the **octave** symbol to avoid excessive use of ledger lines. An octave is the distance between the closest notes of the same name (so-called because the note names recur every eight pitches; "octava" means "eight" in Italian). The most frequent symbol to indicate that a note or notes is to be played or sung at the next *higher* octave is *8va- - - - - - - - - - -*, and it is written above the affected notes. The most frequent symbol to indicate that a note or notes is to be played or sung at the next octave *lower* is *8bassa- - - - - - - - - - -*, or 8vb, and it is written below the affected notes. Note in the example below how much easier it is to read the notes with octave symbols than the notes they represent.

EXAMPLE 1-8 Octave Signs

Accidentals

We have now accounted for the white notes of the piano keyboard and these constitute seven of the twelve possible different pitches typical of Western music. The black keys are named in relationship to the white keys. It is helpful to know at this point that adjacent notes on the piano keyboard are considered to be a **half step** apart from each other. We use **accidentals** to count up or down from a given note. There are five accidentals, which are reproduced in Example 1-9. You will note that they are shown in a diagonal, in a relationship indicating half step relationships from the lowest (double flat) to the highest (double sharp) accidental.

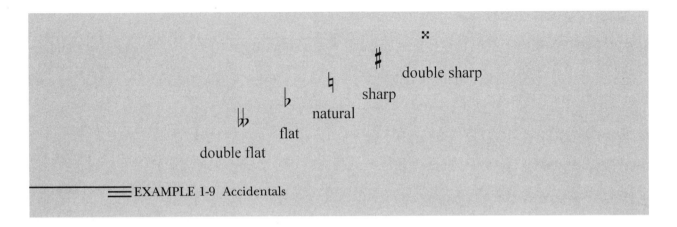

EXAMPLE 1-9 Accidentals

We can move up a half step to the next adjacent note from any note by moving up the diagonal of symbols. Changing a flat note to natural, for example, moves it up a half step to the adjacent note. Conversely, we can move down a half step by using the symbol descending in the chart above. Changing a double sharp to a sharp note, for example, moves the note to the adjacent tone below it. The black notes on the keyboard can be named in relationship to the lower white note name (in which case we add a sharp), or in relationship to the upper white note (in which case we add a flat). On the keyboard below, notice the names of the black notes. When we move up from "c" to the black note immediately adjacent above it, we use a sharp to indicate it. Similarly, we can name the same note "d flat" if we describe it as a half step below "d." Whether called "c#" or "db," we are speaking of the same note on the piano.

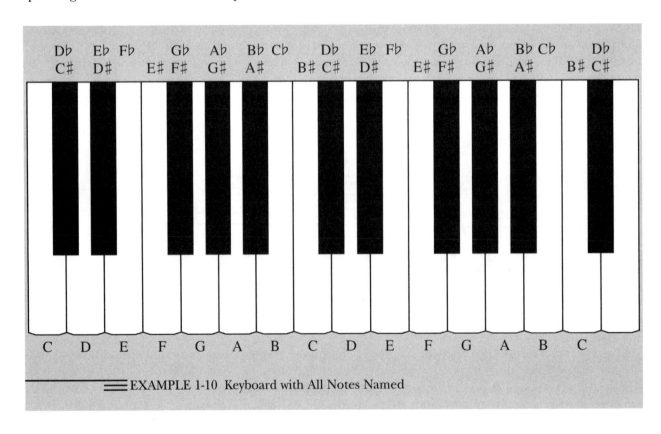

EXAMPLE 1-10 Keyboard with All Notes Named

White notes too can be named in relation to other white notes, as we will discover when we explore keys. The note "b" can also be named "a" double sharp or "c" flat. "F" can also be named "e" sharp" or "g" double flat. Two or more names for the same pitch are called **enharmonics** or **enharmonic equivalents.** The following groups of notes illustrate enharmonic equivalents. All three pitches of any group refer to the same note on the piano. We will discover the necessity of having different names for the same pitch when we explore keys in Chapter 4.

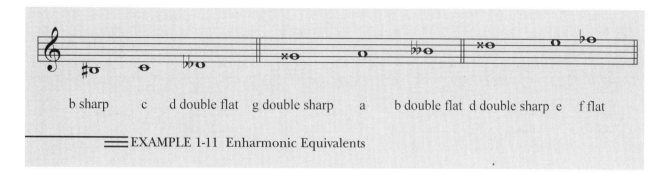

b sharp   c   d double flat   g double sharp   a   b double flat   d double sharp   e   f flat

EXAMPLE 1-11 Enharmonic Equivalents

Diatonic Half Steps and Whole Steps

The term **diatonic** refers to the materials used to produce a certain style of tonal music. In Chapter 4, we will explore scales and keys. For our purposes in learning about diatonic half steps and whole steps, it is sufficient to know that "diatonic" refers to notes with *different* note names. When we speak of diatonic half and whole steps, we are referring to *adjacent* notes with different names ("c" and "d" for example, or "eb" and "f"). As already mentioned, the smallest interval between any two notes of the Western scale is a half step. The distance between "b" and "c," "f" and "gb," and "e" and "f" is a half step, and it is called diatonic because both pitches are adjacent and have adjacent note names.

As we will discover in Chapter 4, this is useful to know in order to learn how to construct **scales,** which are the source materials for much of Western music during the last several hundred years. For the moment, we will content ourselves with learning how to build strings of diatonic whole steps and half steps. We have already discussed half steps, which were defined as adjacent notes on the piano keyboard. For the exercise, we will also have to learn that two-half steps equals a **whole step.**

Following the steps below will ensure that you can build diatonic whole and half steps.

Task 1: Write two consecutive **diatonic whole steps** above the given note.

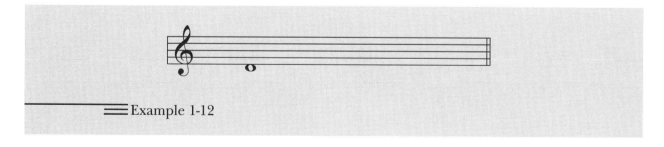

Example 1-12

Step 1: Write the next two note names above the given note and put in the required intervals (1=whole step).

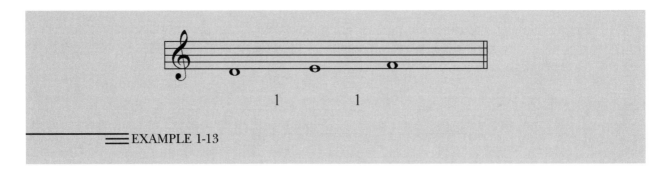

EXAMPLE 1-13

Step 2: Note the pattern of half and whole steps. In this case, you are asked to create consecutive whole steps (represented by the number "1"). Check the keyboard. You will need two half-steps between the first and second notes, and two half-steps between the second and third notes. Using the accidental chart reproduced below, add accidentals to raise or lower notes to make all notes a whole step apart. The accidentals shown below are in half-step increments. To raise a natural note one-half step is to add a sharp. To lower a natural note one-half step is to add a flat. In this case, "d" to "e" IS a whole-step (d to eb is one half-step, eb to e is the second), so we do not need to alter that note. From "e" to "f" is a half-step, and we are asked for a whole step. To make the "f" a half-step higher, we need to raise it from a natural (implied when there is no symbol) to a sharp note.

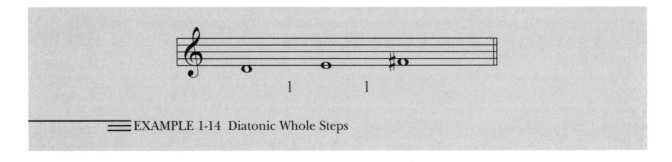

EXAMPLE 1-14 Diatonic Whole Steps

Now if you look at the keyboard, you will see that "d" to "e" is a whole step, and "e" to "f" sharp is a whole step.

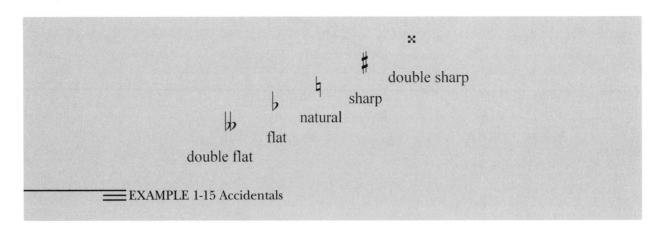

EXAMPLE 1-15 Accidentals

Task 2: Write two consecutive **diatonic half-steps** above the given note.

EXAMPLE 1-16

Step 1: Write the next two note names above the given note and put in the required intervals (1/2=half-step).

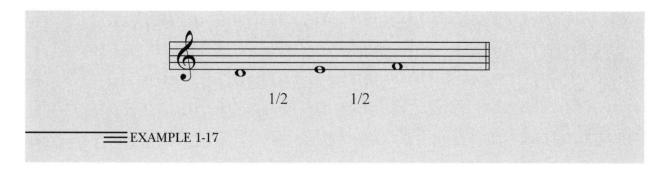

1/2   1/2

EXAMPLE 1-17

Step 2: Note the pattern of half and whole steps. In this case, you are asked to create consecutive half steps (represented by the number 1/2.) You will need one half-step between the first and second notes, and one half-step between the second and third notes. Looking at your keyboard, note that the distance between "d" and "e" is a whole step. To decrease the size of that interval by a half step, the "e" natural must be lowered one-half step. To lower a natural a half-step, we add a flat. Now the distance between "eb" and "f" is a whole step. To bring the "f" a half-step closer to "e," we must also add a flat. Now look at the keyboard. You will see that the three notes, "d," "eb," "fb," are in half- step relationship to each other. (Please observe that accidentals may be used in conjunction with white notes, just as with black notes. "Fb" and "b#" are enharmonic spellings of "e" and "c.")

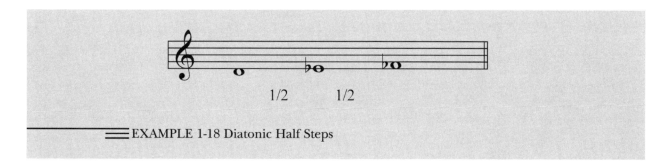

1/2   1/2

EXAMPLE 1-18 Diatonic Half Steps

Task 3: Write a diatonic whole- and half-step above the given note.

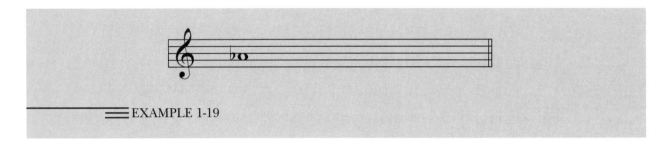

EXAMPLE 1-19

Step 1: Write the next two note names above the given note and put in the required intervals (whole-step and half-step).

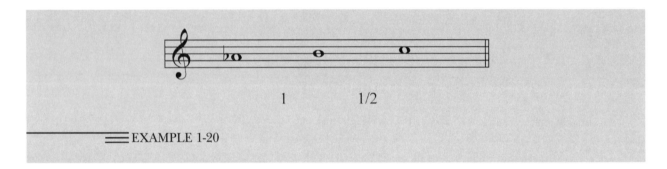

1   1/2

EXAMPLE 1-20

Step 2: Note the pattern of half- and whole-steps. In this case, you are asked to create a consecutive whole-step and half-step. You will need one whole-step between the first and second notes, and one half-step between the second and third notes. Looking at your keyboard, note that the distance between "ab" and "b" is three half-steps. You'll need to reduce that to two half-steps. To lower a natural note by a half-step, add a flat. Now the distance between "bb" and "c" is a whole-step, and you are asked for a half-step. To lower the natural "c" a half-step, you add a flat. Now the required pattern of whole-step/half-step is correctly realized. Look at those notes on your keyboard.

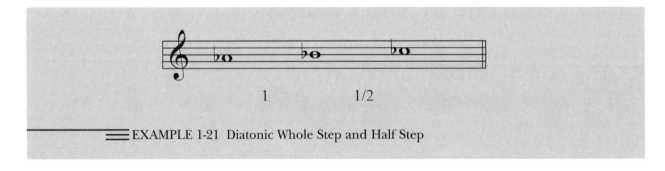

1   1/2

EXAMPLE 1-21 Diatonic Whole Step and Half Step

You now have the skill you need to construct pitches a half-step and whole-step apart. This will enable us to build scales in Chapter 4.

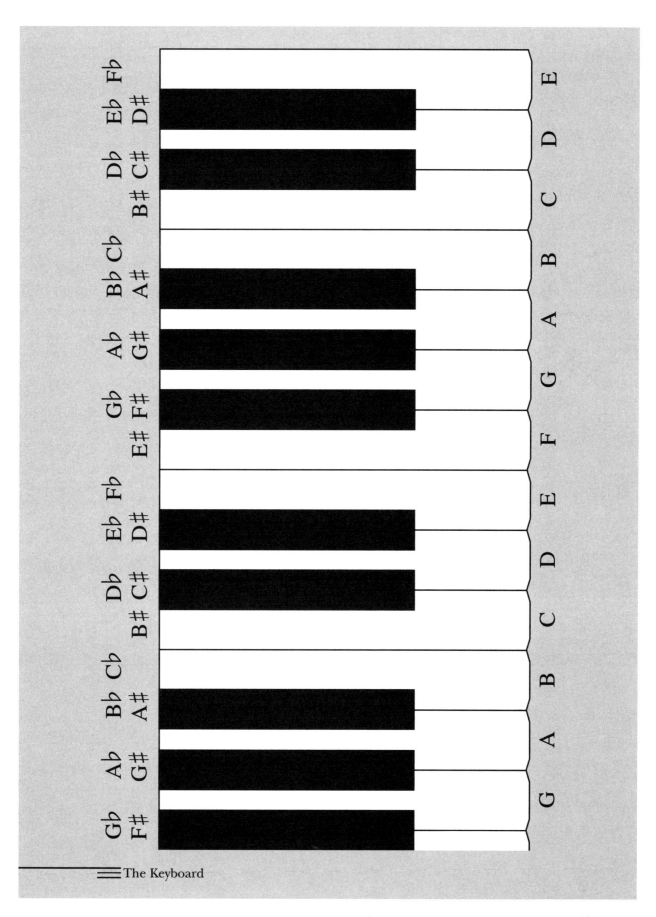

The Keyboard

EXERCISE 1-A

Name: Mike Andreani

Name the notes below. You are given the first three notes for each new clef as examples.

F B♯ E♭ C♯ D A♭ C D♯
G F♯ F D A♭ C♭ G♭ E
F E♯ A C♭ F♯ C♯ G A
E B♭ F♯ A♭ B G♯ C F
A D♯ E♭ A♯ C♯ D C D
B♭ E♯ B♭ E D♭ B♯ G♭ C
C♯ E E♭ G C G♭ B♯ B♯
E A♯ G♭ A B♯ E G♯ G

EXERCISE 1-B

Name:_____

Name the notes below.

C   G♯   G♭

A♭   C♯   B   F   G   D   E   D

E♭   C♯   F   G   A   B   D   C

E♭   G   B   D   G   F   C   A

F♯   A   D   A   B   C   E   G

Write the notes indicated within the staff. (Do not use ledger lines.)

Write note names under the notes as indicated.

C C E G

A   B C A

EXERCISE 1-C

Name:_____

Write two consecutive diatonic whole-steps above the given notes.

Example

     1   1

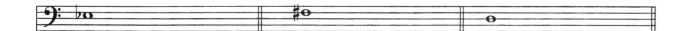

Write two consecutive diatonic half-steps above the given notes.

Example

   1/2   1/2

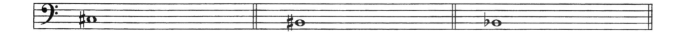

Write a consecutive diatonic whole-step and half-step (in that order) above the given notes.

Example

   1   1/2

Write one enharmonic note for each of the notes given below.

Rhythm, Time, and Meter

Music is a **temporal** art; it unfolds over time, unlike spatial arts like painting, in which one can see a work of art immediately in its entirely, even if understanding occurs over time. There are several definitions of **rhythm,** but for our purposes, rhythm may be defined as **duration:** how long a sound lasts. We have examined pitch. Now we examine rhythm, which defines not only the length of individual notes but also contributes to the character of a piece or section of music.

Symbols represent note durations, and notes, as we have seen in Chapter 1, are ellipses on the staff. These ellipses may be open or filled in. They may have **stems** attached to them, and attached to the stems may be **flags** or **beams.** Open and filled-in notes, flags or no flags, and the number of flags or beams indicate different durations. When there are stems, composers put the stems facing upward for all notes lower than the second space from the bottom of the staff. For all notes starting on the third space from the bottom, the stems face down. If a note is on the middle line, the stem may face up or down. Furthermore, when the stems face up, they are placed to the right of the note; when they face down, they are placed on the left side of the note. When notes that are beamed fall above and below the middle line, the stems are placed according to where the majority of the notes lie. Beams and flags are interchangeable. Composers use beams to attach notes, and flags to keep them separate. (We'll learn below what the beams and flags represent.) The value of a note that has two flags extending from the stem is the same as a note with two beams connected to another note, and this is the case with all flagged and beamed notes. See Examples 2-1 and 2-2.

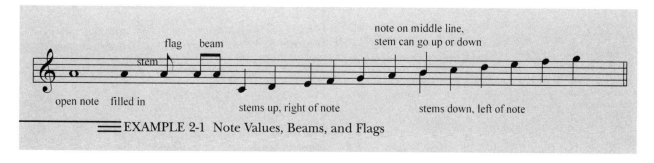

EXAMPLE 2-1 Note Values, Beams, and Flags

EXAMPLES 2-2 Beams and Flags

NOTE VALUES

Note values are proportional and systematic. Once you know what the relationship of one durational symbol is to another, reading rhythm is straightforward and a function of practice. The two charts below demonstrate the relationship of durations to each other. We'll begin with the whole note. As you see in the first chart below, the whole note is worth two half notes, the half note is worth two quarter notes, the quarter note is worth two eighth notes, and so on. The first chart shows the proportions in relationship to each other, the second chart shows the number of notes of lesser value that comprise a whole note.

Name	Note	Value
Whole note	o	1
Half note	♩ or ♩	½
Quarter note	♩ or ♩	¼
Eighth note	♪ or ♪	⅛
Sixteenth note	♬ or ♬	1/16
Thirty-second note	♬ or ♬	1/32

EXAMPLE 2-3 Table of Note Values

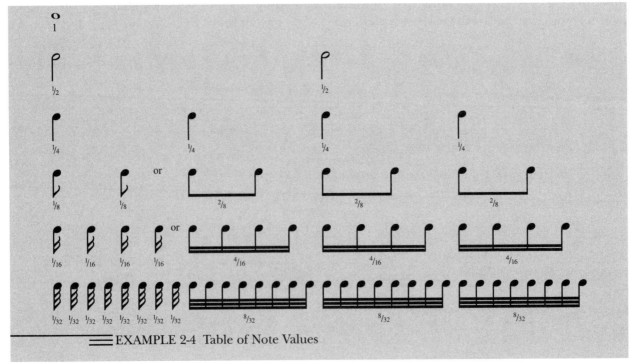

EXAMPLE 2-4 Table of Note Values

Meter

We call a steady and predictable duration between attacks a **pulse** or **beat,** whether explicit or implicit. If you tap on the desk or with your feet in a way that makes each beat follow the previous one after the same time has elapsed, you've created a pulse. Pulses can be very fast, very slow, or anything in between, as we'll discover when we discuss tempo. Composers in the Western world have distinguished between **accented** and **unaccented** beats (beats with greater and lesser stress), and have conceived the groupings of accented and unaccented beats in regular ways. Typically in Western music, the beat in a work is clear. You can tap your foot to it. You'll also notice if you listen closely to a song or piece that there seems to be a beat with a stronger stress, followed by notes with less stress. Typically, there is an accented beat and either one, two, or three unaccented beats following, and this pattern typically persists throughout a piece or a section of a piece. A group of accented beats followed by unaccented beats is "collected" into something called a **measure,** or **bar,** so named because of the line (called a **barline**) that separates measures from each other. The first beat in every measure will get a distinguishing stress. In measures with four beats, the first beat will get a strong stress, and the third beat will get a weaker stress, with beats two and four being unstressed.

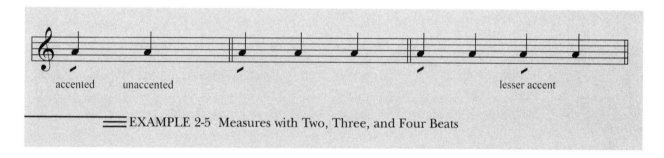

accented   unaccented   lesser accent

EXAMPLE 2-5 Measures with Two, Three, and Four Beats

Meter is the grouping of accented and unaccented beats, that is, the total number of beats per measure and what note value is assigned the beat. Two numbers, called the **meter signature,** are used to indicate the meter: the bottom note indicates what duration gets the beat, while the top number indicates how many beats there are per measure. A 4 as the bottom number indicates that the quarter note gets the beat, a 2 indicates that the half note gets the beat, while an 8 indicates that the eighth note gets the beat. The quarter note is most typically the duration that gets the beat, although those mentioned above are also used, and even meters where the sixteenth or the whole note get the beat occur from time to time. However, when you are figuring out meter, your first choice should be assigning the beat to the quarter note. As stated above, the top note tells the performer how many beats there will be in the measure. Three-four time (we state the top number first) is a measure in which there are three beats and the quarter note gets the beat, while in four-four time there are four beats per measure and the quarter note gets the beat. Two-two time means that there are two beats per measure, and the half note gets the beat, while seven-four means that there are seven beats in a measure and that the quarter note gets the beat. The beat pattern provides the "skeleton" or metric underpinning against which the more individual durations of a melody and other musical lines are juxtaposed. Sometimes the beat is very explicit, as in rock music and most jazz, but sometimes it is implied and more subtly present. Example 2-6 illustrates typical meter signatures (also called **time signatures**).

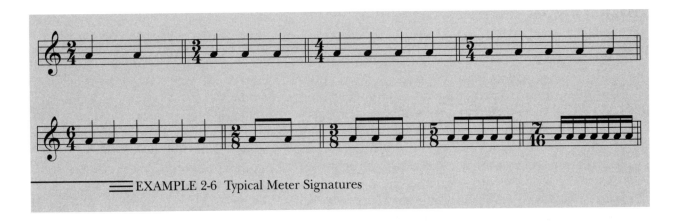

EXAMPLE 2-6 Typical Meter Signatures

Example 2-7 shows melodies in three meters. In the case of the first two examples, the first beat of each measure gets a stress. In the melody in four-four, the first beat gets a substantial stress while the third beat gets a subordinate stress. You'll notice that each bar has note values that add up to the correct number of beats. Against the melody notes in this example, steady quarter note beats are implied.

EXAMPLE 2-7 Melodies in Three Meters

Ties and Dots

Ties connect the noteheads of two or more notes to each other and indicate that the tied notes are not to be rearticulated. In the example below, all of the durations are exactly the same, although they are notated differently. Ties are used to connect held notes from measure to measure, when it is not possible to write a duration using one note, and to make notation easier to read.

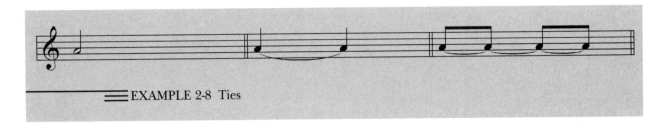

EXAMPLE 2-8 Ties

Dots, sometimes called augmentation dots, add half the value of a note to its duration. For example, a quarter note with a dot is the equivalent duration of a quarter note **tied** to an eighth note. A note with two dots adds half the value of the note, and half the value of the first dot. For example, a quarter note with two dots spells a duration that is equal to a quarter note, plus an eighth note, plus a sixteenth note. (Ties connect notes; tied notes are not reattacked.)

EXAMPLE 2-9 Dots

Note in the first example below the use of dots to simplify the notation and to extend notes beyond a beat. The second line shows the same rhythm without dots. The first example is less cluttered than the second. As for ties, observe that the first duration in the last measure is not possible *without* the use of a tie, as there is no single durational symbol that equals five sixteenth notes.

EXAMPLE 2-10 Rhythm Example with Dots and Ties

Duple and Triple Meters

Most Western music has been written in units in which there are two beats, four beats, or three beats per measure. Meters that are based on two (two, four, or less typically eight) beats are called **duple meters.** Meters that are based on three beats per measure are called **triple meters.**

Simple Meter

In a **simple meter,** the beat is divided into two equal parts, or parts divisible by two. In the majority of cases, composers choose to represent the beat with a quarter note, which can be broken into two parts (eighth notes), or four parts (sixteenth notes), or various combinations of eighth and sixteenth notes. Example 2-11 illustrates simple meters, with various subdivisions of the beat. The basic beat is shown on the bottom space.

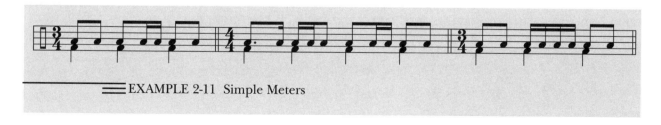

EXAMPLE 2-11 Simple Meters

Compound Meter

In a **compound meter,** the beats are subdivided into three equal parts. As a result, the beat will generally be a dotted note, and the most common beat in a compound meter is the dotted quarter. There is something misleading about compound meters, which are generally "named" for the note of the subdivision rather than for the main beat. For example, in 6/8 time, it is the dotted quarter note that gets the beat. But there is no way to indicate that the dotted quarter gets the beat in the bottom number of the meter signature, so composers do the next best thing. They use the subdivision of the beat as the bottom figure of the meter signature. The typical 6/8 pattern below puts the accent on the first dotted quarter note unit, and a lighter stress on the second dotted quarter note unit.

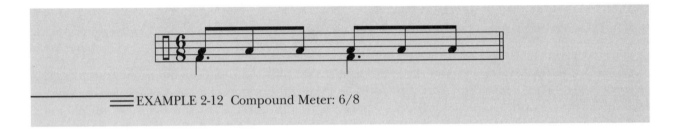

EXAMPLE 2-12 Compound Meter: 6/8

Example 2-13 demonstrates various compound meter signatures. The dotted quarter note gets the beat. The bottom note shows this beat, with various figures on top.

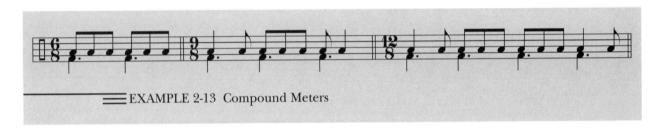

EXAMPLE 2-13 Compound Meters

Telling Simple from Compound Meters

When trying to ascertain whether a beat pattern is in a simple or compound meter, it is necessary to figure out whether each beat is divided into two parts or three parts. For our purposes, a good rule of thumb about whether an unmarked measure is in a simple or compound meter is to see whether the composer has beamed notes in units of two or three. For example, if you were to see six eighth notes without beams, it would be impossible to determine whether the grouping of the notes suggested units of two (simple meter), or units of three (compound meter). However, once the units are beamed, it is easy to tell. In 2-14a, next page, three quarter notes are clearly subdivided into two eighth notes each. This is a simple meter and is called 3/4. In 2-14b, the basic beat is a dotted quarter note, subdivided into three equal parts. Since there is no way to represent a meter signature as 2-dotted quarter notes per bar (since we don't use fractions), we call it 6/8. Even though both measures have the same number of eighth notes, these examples sound quite different, as a simple meter divides the measure into three parts, while a compound meter divides the measure into two parts. In 2-14a, there is a pulse on every quarter note. In 2-14b, there is a pulse on every dotted quarter note. This creates a different effect. (The bottom notes show the basic beat.)

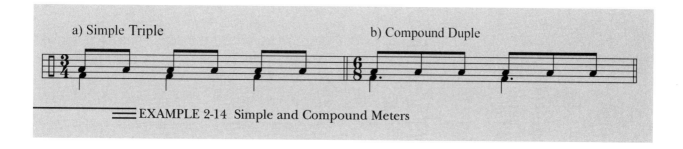

EXAMPLE 2-14 Simple and Compound Meters

When beats are clearly subdivided into three parts, the bottom number of the meter signature should be the note value of the subdivided note. This will usually be an eighth note. Observe the simple and compound meters in Example 2-15. Note once again that in the two simple meters, the basic beat is divisible by two; in the compound meters, the basic beat is divisible by three.

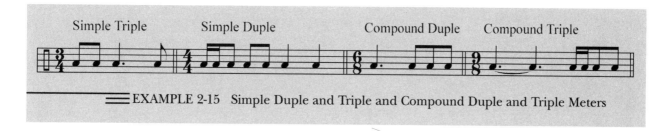

EXAMPLE 2-15 Simple Duple and Triple and Compound Duple and Triple Meters

Rests

Just as there are symbols to indicate the duration of a sound, there are also symbols to indicate the duration of silence. The symbols that tell musicians not to play are called **rests.** The chart in Example 2-16 gives the symbols for the different rests. You'll notice that in the case of eighth, sixteenth, and thirty-second note rests, the number of flags on the stem of the rest is the same as the number of flags for the notes. Rests are useful as part of melodies and accompaniments. In an orchestral score, for example, groups of instruments are silent for many measures at a time. Note that a dot after a rest adds half the value to the rest (for example a dotted quarter note rest is equal to one quarter and one eighth duration of silence). There are also double dotted rests. The first dot adds half of the rest's value, the second dot adds half of that (for example a quarter note rest with two dots would be the equivalent of a quarter, plus an eighth, plus a sixteenth of silence).

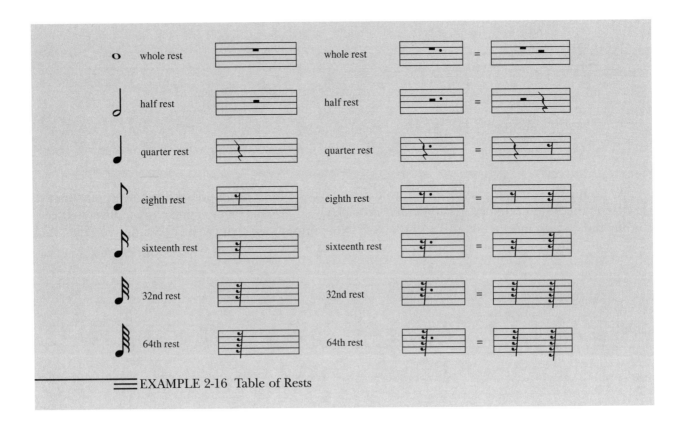

EXAMPLE 2-16 Table of Rests

As you can see in Example 2-17, rests create "spaces" between notes and help to articulate musical phrases.

EXAMPLE 2-17 Melody with Rests

Tuplets

Sometimes a composer wants to "force" more notes into a beat than it can contain—especially when the number of notes doesn't fit evenly into the beat—or subdivide a beat into a number of subdivisions that is not natural to it. For example, we saw that simple meters subdivide beats into units based on two or four. When a composer wants to fit more notes than is natural into a beat, he or she writes what is generically called a **tuplet.** Tuplets are numbers put above or below a collection of notes that tells the performer to "fit" the number of notes into a beat that is too small for it. When one does that with two notes, it is called a **"duplet,"** while three notes is called a **"triplet,"** four a **"quadruplet,"** and five a **"quintuplet."** In Example 2-18, the triplet tells the performer (a) to fit three eighth notes in the time of two eighth notes, (b) to fit four eighth notes in the space of three eighth notes, and (c) to fit five sixteenth notes in the time of four sixteenth notes.

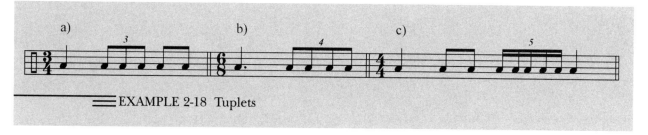

EXAMPLE 2-18 Tuplets

Tempo and Character Markings

Tempo is the speed of the pulse in a piece or section of a piece and was characteristically described in the original modern language of music, Italian. Typical designations describing tempo and character run the gamut from very slow to very fast. Following is a list of some of those Italian designations.

- **Grave: very slow and solemn**
- **Largo: very slow and expressive**
- **Andante: moderate "walking" speed**
- **Moderato: moderate tempo**
- **Allegretto: moderately fast**
- **Allegro: fast**
- **Presto: very fast**

In the nineteenth century, composers began to write tempo and character markings in their native language. **Character marks** help define the spirit of a piece and give hints about how the composer imagines the music's personality. Sometimes these marks also indicate a tempo. *Vivace* (Italian) means "quickly" but also "lively." *Bewegt* (German) means "rather fast" but also connotes "agitation." Many character marks are independent of tempo and there are thousands of such helpful marks in music. Composers may be more or less prescriptive about how they want their music to be performed. Words such as "expressive," "tenderly," "agitated," "fiery," "joyfully," in whatever language, help convey the composer's sense of how he or she would like the music played, and there is a long list of such typical words. Composers sometimes become creative in describing how they want their music to be performed. The Russian composer Alexander Scriabin wrote copious and unusual directions. In his Sixth Piano Sonata, he wrote such instructions as "horror is rising," "undulating," "imperious," "crushing," "thundering," "with painful voluptuousness," and other colorful instructions.

Descriptive tempo and character indications are helpful, if inexact, where the precise speed of the pulse is concerned. In 1816, Johann Malzel invented the metronome, an instrument that could indicate the speed of the pulse in an exact way. The mechanical metronome has a flange with a weight that can be adjusted to indicate how many pulses equal one minute. Quarter note equals 60, a moderate tempo, indicates that each beat should last one second. Quarter note equals 120, a rather brisk tempo, indicates that each quarter note should last for one-half second. Most commonly in music, the quarter note gets the beat, although sometimes the half or eighth note is the unit that gets the beat. Although less descriptive, this more "scientific" way of measuring speed allows composers to convey more exactly the tempo of the music. Metronome indications with character descriptions allow composers to indicate the exact tempo of music as well as its personality, for example with the indication quarter note equals 120, "lively." Such markings are found at the beginning of a score of music, and everywhere the composer wants to indicate a change of tempo or character.

EXERCISE 2-A

fw 2/5

Name: Michael Andreani

Write two of the following pairs of notes, following the first example.
Where possible, write the first pair using flags, the second pair using beams.

eighths   sixteenths   quarters   thirty-seconds

Write the indicated notes.

whole note   half note   quarter note   eighth note   sixteenth note   thirty-second note

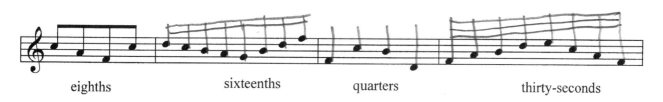

eighths   sixteenths   quarters   thirty-seconds

Write the equivalent rests for the following notes.

Without using dots and by tying notes together,
write the durations for the following dotted notes.

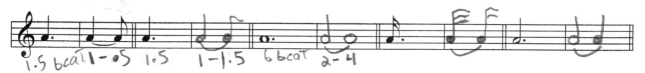

1.5 beat 1-.05 1.5   1-1.5   6 beat   2-4

Write a dotted note for each of the tied notes.

Exercises in Rhythm

The goal of this chapter is to get you to think about rhythm and how to organize rhythmic ideas. Most music has logic and order at its core. We have now learned about the "nuts and bolts" of duration, measures, and meters; now we're going to learn how to organize these elements. You should think about music the way you think about language. Generally, when writing, one strives for clarity of expression and for each sentence to flow to the next logically. Music usually works in the same way. Ideas are developed, flowing logically from the preceding idea.

At the end of this chapter, you will write an eight-measure rhythm exercise. Let's first look at Example 3-1, which is "disorderly." (The bottom notes give the beat.) Certainly, all the durations are correct, and each measure adds up correctly. But you'll notice as you tap or sing it that there is no logic to it, nor much in the way of correspondence between the measures. The measures are like random sentences strung together that have little to do with each other. This example doesn't "compound" into something that makes sense. The choices seem arbitrary and no measure seems to relate to any other. There are six different note values, but no attempt to relate them to each other. For example, there are thirty-second notes in measure 4 but nowhere else, a whole note in measure 6 but nowhere else, and a dotted quarter note in measure 7 but nowhere else. The whole thing doesn't add up to anything comprehensible.

EXAMPLE 3-1

Although sometimes composers want to produce the effect of chaos, most of the time composers strive for coherence. Tap your foot to the beat and tap or sing (on "tah") the top rhythms in Example 3-2. You will note that although there are eight measures, the example can be subdivided into two groups of four measures each, and each four-measure phrase can be further subdivided into two two-measure subphrases. You'll further note that alternating measures, 1, 3, 5, and 7, and 2, 4, 6, and 8, have a certain family resemblance to each other. Measures 1, 3, 5, and 7 all begin with a dotted quarter note, which links those measures together. Measures 2 and 6, the second measure of each four-measure phrase, ends with two eighth notes and a quarter note, and measures 4 and 8, the last measure of each two-measure phrase, has the example's only half notes, creating a sense of relaxation at the end of each phrase. Notice that measure 3 is an elaboration of measure 1, that measure 5 begins much like measure 1 with a slight change and that measure 7 begins like measure 5 but uses faster rhythms. This creates a sense of motion and increased activity just before the relaxed ending.

EXAMPLE 3-2

Example 3-3 has a similar organizational profile. Measures 1, 3, 5, and 7 have elements in common that relate them to each other, including a prominent eighth note on the upbeat of beat 1 of each of those measures (**downbeats** occur at the beginning of beat, **upbeats** take place within, not on, a beat), and a quarter note for beat 4. Measures 2, 4, and 6 are related by the conspicuous half note that ends each measure, decreasing activity. Note that measures 1, 3, 5, and 7 have similar degrees of rhythmic activity, although measures 3 and 5 "comment" on measure 1 and increase the activity slightly. Measures 2, 4, and 6 have a clear progression of increased activity, with measure 8 being the most active rhythmically. The example ends in a flourish, the greatest activity saved for the ending. Tap your foot to the bottom pulse and sing the rhythms on top on "tah."

EXAMPLE 3-3

At the core of much music are time-honored means of creating coherence. Composers strive to repeat musical material, as the mind looks to organize elements (musical or otherwise) into comprehensible patterns. Too much repetition creates redundancy and lack of interest; not enough repetition creates a sense of formlessness or incoherence. Composers often repeat ideas with variation, and part of the fun of informed listening is following how recognizable musical ideas change through the course of a piece. In the two examples above, rhythmic ideas are repeated, elaborated, and varied, and both examples should strike you as having a formal coherence and logic.

EXERCISE 3-A

Name: _____

Tap the beat (steady bottom notes) with your foot while singing (on "tah") the rhythms of the top line. Note that the end of a musical example is indicated by a double bar, a thick black line at the end, preceded by a thin line. Note too the clef at the left of each line. This is the symbol for percussion music, and is used when a specific pitch is not indicated.

Note here that the dotted quarter note in the next two examples gets the beat and each beat is subdivided into units of three eighth notes. These are compound meters.

Scales and Keys

We are concerned in this book with the rudiments of **tonal** music. Historians and theorists agree that music of the Renaissance period moved gradually toward the development of **tonality** as music's central system by the beginning of the 1600s, and that system developed until the end of the nineteenth century. By the beginning of the twentieth century, the most advanced composers were looking for alternatives to the tonal system and developed often elaborate new ways to construct music. Nevertheless, throughout the century some composers continued to rely on the tonal system to anchor their music, and tonality enjoyed a resurgence toward the end of the century. Whatever the experiments and discoveries of classical composers of the twentieth- and now twenty-first centuries, most of the music we hear, including jazz, rock, soul, film, folk, and popular music, and some music by classical composers, is in the tonal tradition. Therefore, understanding the foundations of tonal music will give us insight into much of the music that we hear.

Tonal music is a system in which a specific tone acts as a "home," or **tonic**, note. The materials of tonal music create a gravitational pull back to the tonic. There are twelve different notes between any note and the same named note in the next higher and lower register. Composers of tonal music make a **scale**—which is a succession of notes a half or whole step apart from each other—out of seven of the possible twelve notes and construct music confined to their use in a given section of a piece. The seven notes of a given scale form the foundation for both the melodies and the **harmony** (notes played in combination with each other) of a section of music.

SCALES

When we speak of the tonal system, we are referring to a way of organizing music that makes the tonic note (the first note of the scale) the most important tone, and the tone to which all other pitches are subordinate and to which they gravitate. Tonality makes great use of the tension and release that results from the organization of the tonic note and the other notes of a scale. The gravitational pull back to tonic can be easily perceived if we look at any tonal scale. If you play the seven notes of the C Major scale, reproduced below, stopping on "b," you should have a sense of tension and irresolution. Since "b" gravitates to "c," the tonic of the C Major scale, the scale seems unresolved if we pause on "b." Now go back and play the seven notes of the scale and conclude on "c" and you will feel a strong sense of resolution and finality. Tonal scales are created to produce this gravitational pull back to the tonic. At the heart of tonal music, on the local and larger architectural level, is the tension and release that is central to the tonal system. In every tonal scale, the first degree of the scale is labeled scale degree 1 and each pitch above that note is numbered consecutively. Scale degrees also have names, which are labeled above the staff in Example 4-1, with the scale degree numerals listed beneath the staff.

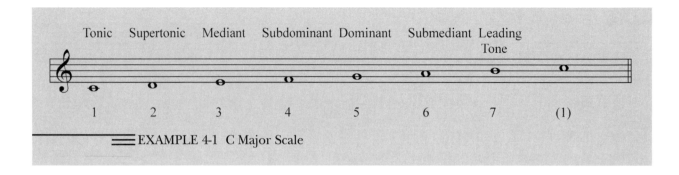

EXAMPLE 4-1 C Major Scale

The tonal system makes use of two primary modes, or kinds of scales, and they are called **major** and **minor.** Each has its own organization of half and whole steps, and while one might not expect the slight difference of a half- or whole-step here or there to have such a profound effect on the character of the sound, in fact major and minor scales, and the music they create, do have entirely different characters.

THE MAJOR SCALE

The pattern of whole and half steps that form the major scale is as follows:

1   1   1/2   1   1   1   1/2

If you begin on any note on the keyboard or another instrument and construct a pattern of whole and half steps in the order above, you will produce a **Major Scale.** Let's look again at the C Major scale, taking note of the relationship between each consecutive note of the scale. If you look at your keyboard, you'll see that the pattern of whole and half steps is exactly that of the pattern given above. We observe then that when we play a scale from C to C, playing each white note, we wind up with a C Major scale.

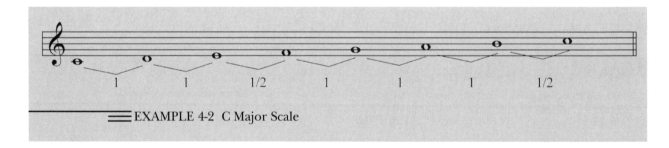

EXAMPLE 4-2 C Major Scale

Let's take a look at another scale, G major.

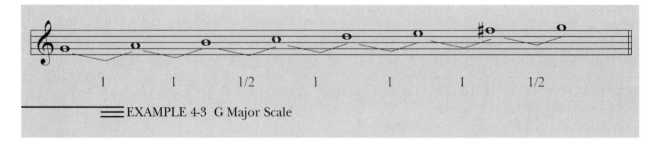

EXAMPLE 4-3 G Major Scale

We now note that when we start on G and construct the major scale, "f" must be raised to "f" sharp to create the pattern of whole and half steps that produce the major scale. C Major was the scale or **key** (we refer to the specific notes of any major or minor scale as its "key") with no sharps or flats, while G Major is the key with "f" sharp and all the other notes natural.

Here is an F Major scale:

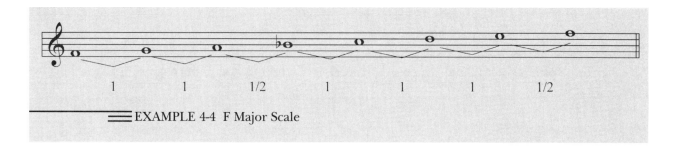

EXAMPLE 4-4 F Major Scale

We note now that when we start on "f" and follow the pattern of whole and half steps for the major scale, all notes are natural except for "b," which is flat. Take a look at your keyboard and follow the pattern of whole steps and half steps.

This is a good point at which to make some observations about scales. Note that there are seven pitches before the first, or tonic, note is repeated. Observe too that until the repeated note, every one of the note names (a, b, c, d, e, f, g) appears once, and once only, whether as a natural, sharp, or flat note. In other words, there will never be two of the same note names (for example, "a" flat and "a" sharp) in any scale, nor will any note name ever be omitted. Furthermore, a major scale can be built on every one of the twelve notes of the chromatic scale (all the notes between "c" and "b" consecutively). In following the pattern of whole and half steps, every scale will have a *different* combination of natural, flat, and sharp notes. Major scales can have natural *and* sharp notes, natural and flat notes, all flat notes, or all sharp notes, but they will never have both sharp and flat notes.

Let's practice constructing major scales by following the steps outlined below. Immediately following, you will have an opportunity to practice forming a major scale, and your homework assignment at the end of this chapter will give you additional practice in doing so.

Constructing an E Major Scale

Beginning on the tonic note, write all of the note names from "e" to "e." Remember, there must be one of each note name and only one until you get to the repeat of the tonic note. (Writing all the note names before you begin to alter pitches will save a lot of confusion and errors later.)

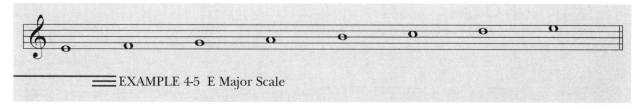

EXAMPLE 4-5 E Major Scale

Now that you've written all the note names, add the sequence of whole and half steps below the scale in the order 1-1-1/2-1-1-1-1/2. Use carets to show that the interval is between the two notes indicated.

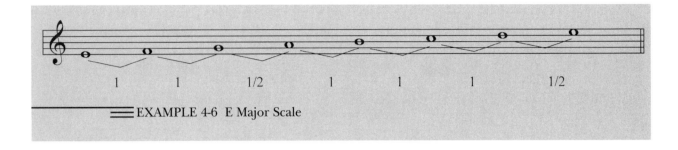

EXAMPLE 4-6 E Major Scale

Checking your keyboard, alter the notes according to the interval pattern, raising natural notes by adding a sharp.

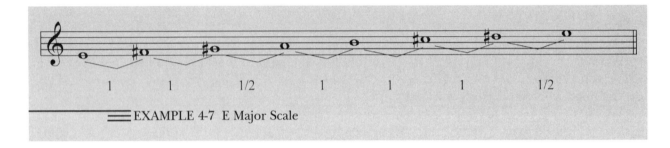

EXAMPLE 4-7 E Major Scale

You have now constructed an E Major scale, which you'll note has four sharps.

Following the same steps, construct the scale for Gb Major. Begin by writing all the note names from "g" flat to "g" flat. Note that the second tonic note of the scale must also have an accidental symbol if the first one does. Since "g" is flat at the bottom of your scale, it must be flat at the top as well. Remember that when you lower a natural note by a half step, you add a flat. Note too that your two tonic notes should agree.

Write in a scale of every note name beginning and ending on Gb.

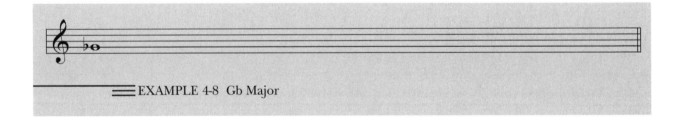

EXAMPLE 4-8 Gb Major

Now reproduce the eight notes and put in the carets and interval pattern under the pitches.

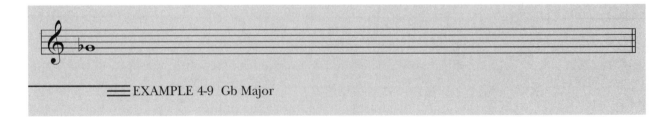

EXAMPLE 4-9 Gb Major

Now reproduce your pitches in the interval pattern 1-1-1/2-1-1-1-1/2, looking at your keyboard to alter the pitches. Remember that when you lower a natural note by a half step, you add a flat.

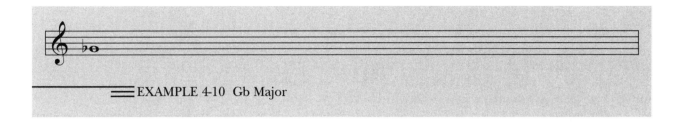

EXAMPLE 4-10 Gb Major

Major Key Signatures

Now that you understand how the major scale is made, we can look at the shortcuts composers have used to indicate a key without having to write measure after measure of accidentals. We've observed the number of flats or sharps in several scales (or keys). We've seen that C Major has no flats or sharps, G Major has one sharp, E Major has four sharps, F Major has one flat, and Gb major has six flats. By reproducing all of the sharps or flats in a given key at the beginning of the staff, the composer is telling the performer that every time he or she comes upon that note—"f" sharp or "b" flat, for example—the note is to be played as a sharp or a flat, no matter what the register. The collection of flats or sharps at the beginning of a staff is called the **key signature**, which tells the performer to play a given note as sharp or flat as indicated.

Note the key signatures for the five scales we've produced so far.

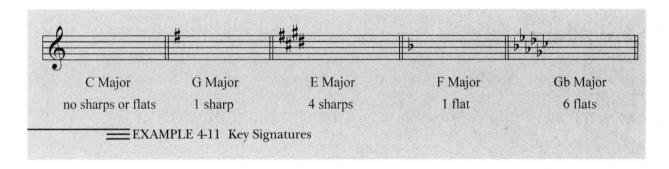

C Major	G Major	E Major	F Major	Gb Major
no sharps or flats	1 sharp	4 sharps	1 flat	6 flats

EXAMPLE 4-11 Key Signatures

The short tune below is in E Major, which is indicated by the key signature of four sharps preceding the music. This tells the performer that when he or she sees the notes "f," "c," "g," or "d," they are to be played as "f" sharp, "c" sharp, "g" sharp, and "d" sharp.

E G# B B   C# A B   E   D# C# B A G# F#   E G# F# D# E

EXAMPLE 4-12 E Major Melody

Music is very systematic in the way keys work, and it is therefore possible to learn how key signatures operate. As we've seen, the key of C major has no sharps or flats, the key of G has one sharp. To this we can add that the key of D has two sharps, the key of A has three sharps, and, as we have seen, the key of E has four sharps. When we add sharps, we add them to the sharps we've already seen in each preceding key. In other words, G Major has one sharp, "f" sharp. D Major has two sharps, "f" sharp and "c" sharp. A Major has three sharps, "f" sharp, "c" sharp, and "g" sharp, while E Major has four sharps, "f" sharp, "c" sharp, "g" sharp, and "d" sharp. If you learn the order of sharps—F, C, G, D, A, E, B—you will find it easy to write key signatures. The key with one sharp has an "f" sharp; the key with two sharps, "f" sharp and "c" sharp; the key with three sharps, "f" sharp, "c" sharp, and "g" sharp, and so on. Some students remember the sharps by remembering the mnemonic "**F**at **C**ats **G**o **D**own **A**nd **E**at **B**irds."

Just as the order of sharps is consistent and inviolable, so is the order of flats. C Major has no flats or sharps; F Major has one flat, "b"; Bb Major has two flats, "b" flat and "e" flat; Eb Major has three flats, "b" flat, "e" flat, and "a" flat, and so on. For each new key, we add a flat to the previous group of flats. The key with one flat has "b" flat; the key with two flats has "b" flat and "e" flat; the key with three flats has "b" flat, "e" flat, "a" flat, and so on. Here too we will find it profitable to learn the order of flats in the key signature. They are the "retrograde" (the reverse order) of the sharps. If you learn the order of sharps and then write them from last note to first, you will have the order of flats.

Order of sharps and flats in the key signature:

F sharp	C sharp	G sharp	D sharp	A sharp	E sharp	B sharp
B flat	E flat	A flat	D flat	G flat	C flat	F flat

Now we must learn where the flats and sharps go on the treble and bass clefs. Study the order of flats and sharps in both clefs. You must memorize this. Your teacher will show you an easy way to learn the pattern, which is the same for flats in bass and treble clefs, and for sharps in bass and treble clefs.

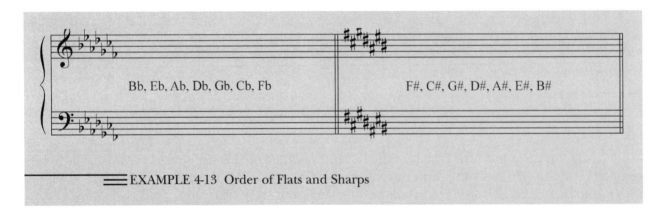

Bb, Eb, Ab, Db, Gb, Cb, Fb   F#, C#, G#, D#, A#, E#, B#

EXAMPLE 4-13 Order of Flats and Sharps

The Major Key Circle of Fifths

Tonal music is systematic. If you start on "c" and go up five scale steps, you will arrive at "g." If you create a scale on "g," you will discover that the key of G Major has one sharp. If you go up five scale steps from "g" to "d," and start a new major scale on "d," you will see that another sharp is added. As you travel up five scale degrees from key to key, you will discover that each new key maintains the previous sharps and adds a new one. G Major has one sharp—"f" sharp. D Major has two sharps: "f" sharp and "c" sharp. The key of A Major has three sharps: "f" sharp, "c" sharp, and "g" sharp, and so on until we reach the key of C sharp Major, which contains seven sharps. Look at the **Major Key Circle of Fifths** on the next page and read clockwise from the key of C Major to observe all the sharp keys.

Keys with flats work similarly. As the circle of fifths travels from C Major counterclockwise, flats are added one flat at a time, each one five scale degrees **down** from each previous key. The key of F Major has one flat, "b" flat. The key of Bb adds a second flat, and contains "b" flat and "e" flat, while the key of Eb adds a third flat to the previous two, so that its key signature contains "b" flat, "e" flat, and "a" flat. This pattern of adding flats one at a time counterclockwise around the circle of fifths continues until we reach the key of seven flats, C flat Major. Note that the keys after F Major going counterclockwise are all "flat keys," that is, the keyname has a flat in it: Bb, Eb, Ab, Db, Gb, Cb.

Study the Major Key Circle of Fifths. You'll notice that there are seven "sharp" keys (keys with sharps in the key signature) and seven "flat" keys (keys with flats in the key signature), and that three keys "overlap" and are enharmonic with each other. F sharp major and G flat major each have six accidentals in the key signature. B Major has five sharps and C flat Major has seven flats. C sharp Major has seven sharps and Db Major has five flats. Because the number of flats and sharps in these keys is almost equal, composers can choose either one of the overlapping keys in which to write pieces, or sections of pieces. These "overlapping" keys are called **enharmonic keys.**

In the space below, write the seven flats in the key signature in treble and bass clef and then the seven sharps. It is important to memorize the order and placement of the accidentals in the key signature. (See Example 4-13 to check your work.)

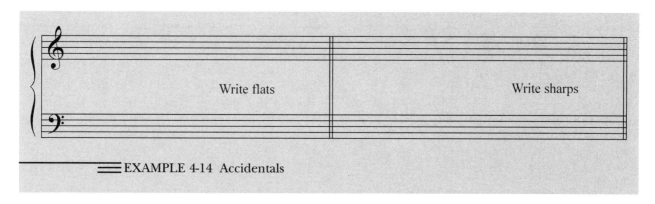

EXAMPLE 4-14 Accidentals

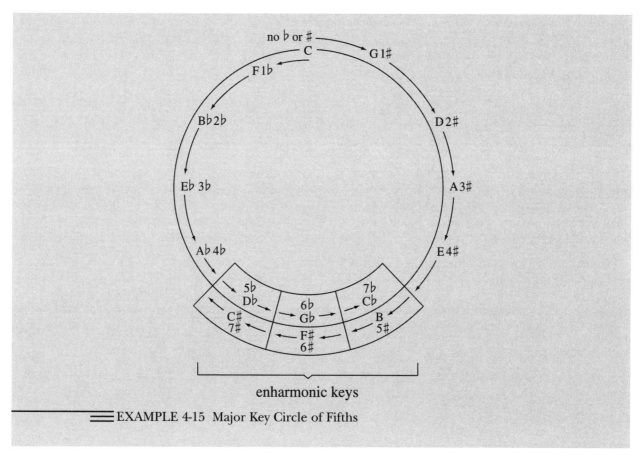

EXAMPLE 4-15 Major Key Circle of Fifths

By referring to the major key circle of fifths, you can get the number of sharps or flats in any key. By memorizing the order of sharps and flats and placing them in their correct positions on the treble and bass clef staff, you can supply the key signature for any key requested. In the example below, add the key signature for the keys indicated and indicate the tonic note. You will need to refer to the Major Key Circle of Fifths and order of sharps and flats (above). The first one is given as an example.

Db Major   C# Major   Bb Major   F# Major

EXAMPLE 4-16 Writing Major Key Signatures

Minor Scales

Major and minor scales have a different pattern of whole- and half-steps. The pattern for the **natural minor** scale is:

$$1 \quad 1/2 \quad 1 \quad 1 \quad 1/2 \quad 1 \quad 1$$

If you begin on any note on the keyboard or another instrument and construct a pattern of whole and half steps in the order above, you will produce a **Natural Minor Scale.** Let's look at the A minor scale, taking note of the relationship between each consecutive note of the scale. If you look at your keyboard, you'll see that the pattern of whole and half steps is exactly that of the pattern given above. We observe then that when we play a scale from "a" to "a," playing each white note, we produce an A minor scale.

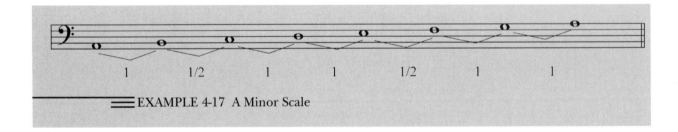

1   1/2   1   1   1/2   1   1

EXAMPLE 4-17 A Minor Scale

Let's take a look at another scale, E minor.

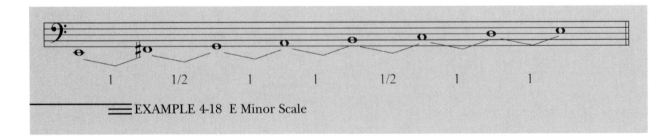

1   1/2   1   1   1/2   1   1

EXAMPLE 4-18 E Minor Scale

When we start on "e" and build the minor scale pattern of whole- and half-steps, "f" must be raised to "f" sharp. "A" minor was the scale or key with no flats or sharps, and E minor is the key with one sharp.

Here is a D Minor scale:

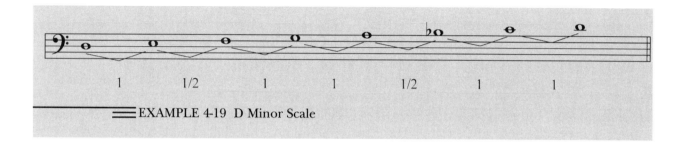

EXAMPLE 4-19 D Minor Scale

We note now that when we start on "d" and follow the pattern of whole and half steps for the minor scale, all notes are natural except for "b," which is flat. Take a look at your keyboard and follow the pattern of whole steps and half steps.

Let's practice constructing minor scales by following the steps outlined below. Immediately following, you will have an opportunity to practice forming a minor scale, and your homework assignment at the end of this chapter will give you additional practice in doing so.

Constructing an F Minor Scale

Beginning on the tonic note, write all of the note names from "f" to "f." Remember, there must be one of each note name and only one until you get to the repeat of the tonic note.

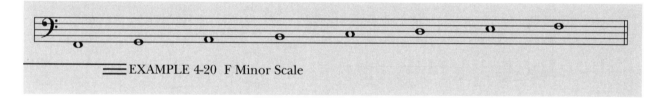

EXAMPLE 4-20 F Minor Scale

Now that you've written all the note names, add the sequence of whole and half steps below the scale. Use carets to show that the interval is between the two notes indicated.

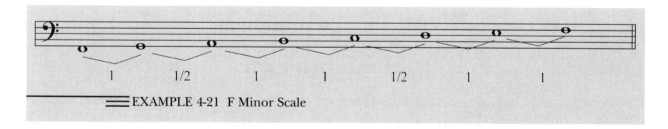

EXAMPLE 4-21 F Minor Scale

Checking your keyboard, alter the notes according to the interval pattern, lowering natural notes by adding a flat.

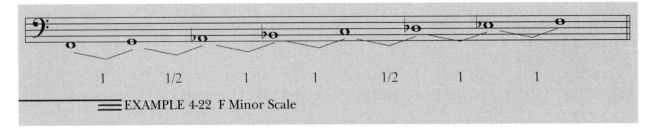

EXAMPLE 4-22 F Minor Scale

You have now constructed an F minor scale, which contains four flats.

Following the same steps, construct the scale for C# minor. Begin by writing all the note names from "c" sharp to "c" sharp. Remember that the second tonic note of the scale must also have an accidental symbol if the first one does. Since "c" is sharp at the bottom of the scale, it must be sharp at the top as well. Remember that when you raise a natural note by a half step, you add a sharp.

Write a scale of every note name beginning and ending on C#.

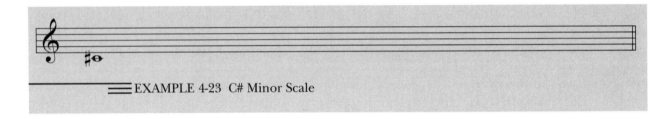

EXAMPLE 4-23 C# Minor Scale

Now reproduce the eight notes and put in the carets and interval pattern under the pitches.

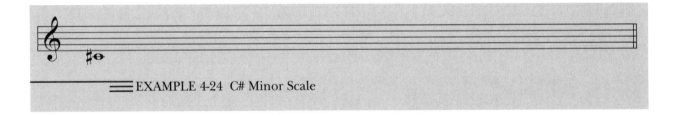

EXAMPLE 4-24 C# Minor Scale

Now reproduce your pitches and interval pattern 1-1/2-1-1-1/2-1-1, looking at your keyboard to alter pitches. Remember that when you raise a natural note by a half step, you add a sharp.

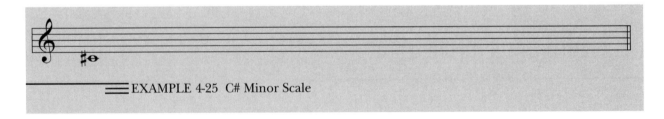

EXAMPLE 4-25 C# Minor Scale

Minor Key Signatures

As with major keys, each minor key has its unique key signature. The key of A minor has no flats or sharps, E minor has one sharp, B minor has two sharps, D minor has one flat, G minor has two flats, and so on. If you look at the **Minor Key Circle of Fifths** below, you will see that it is set up exactly as the Major Key Circle of Fifths insofar as the top key has no flats or sharps and each new key adds one sharp per key going clockwise, and one flat per key going counterclockwise. The difference though is that whereas C Major was the key at the top of the Major Key Circle of Fifths, A minor is the key at the top of the Minor Key Circle of Fifths. These are the keys in major and minor with no sharps or flats. As both circles of fifths organize keys that are five scale steps apart, the keys for the minor key circle of fifths is oriented around A minor rather than C Major, and the keys are adjusted accordingly.

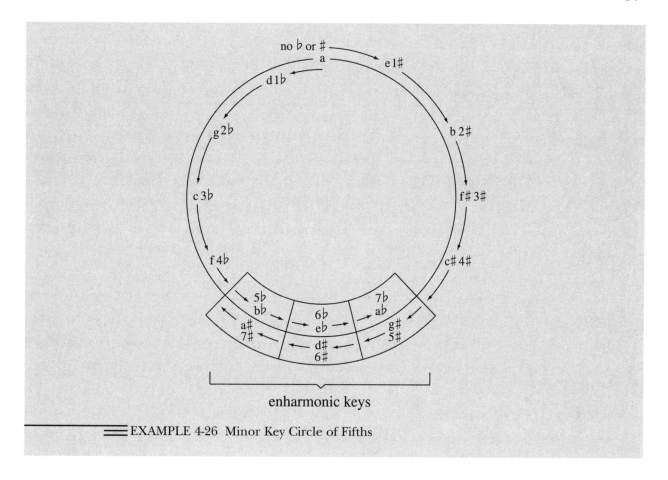

EXAMPLE 4-26 Minor Key Circle of Fifths

By referring to the Minor Key Circle of Fifths, you can get the number of sharps or flats in any key. As you did for the major keys, by memorizing the order of sharps and flats and placing them in their correct positions on the treble and bass clef staffs, you can supply the key signature for any minor key requested. In Example 4-27, add the key signature and a tonic note for the keys indicated. The first one is given as an example.

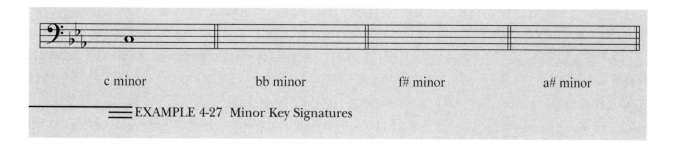

c minor   bb minor   f# minor   a# minor

EXAMPLE 4-27 Minor Key Signatures

Below are the Circle of Fifths for major and minor keys. Take a moment to compare the two. On the side of the page is the correct order for flats and sharps in treble and bass clefs.

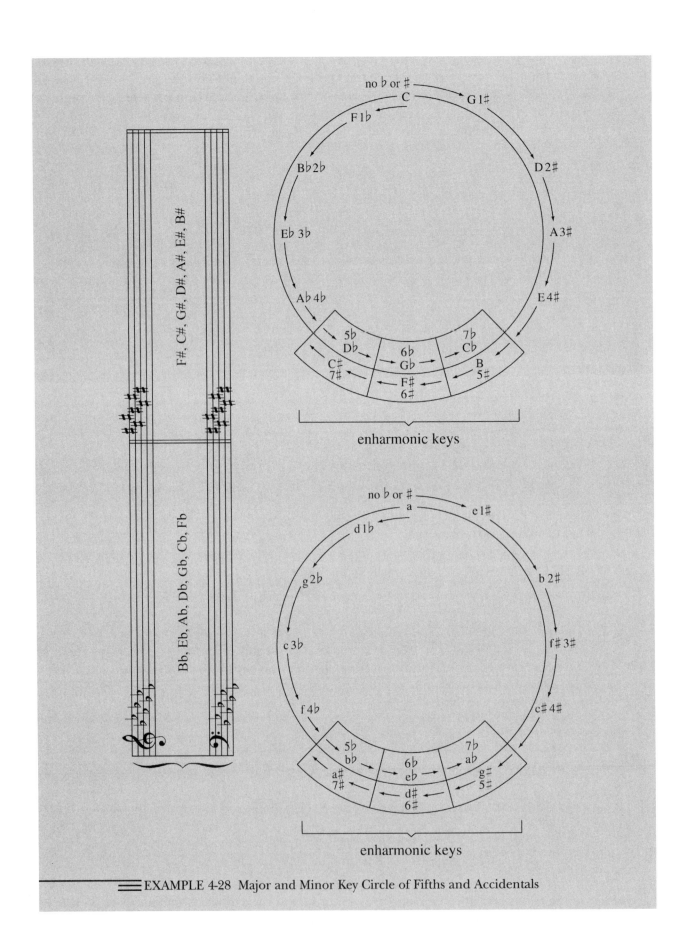

EXAMPLE 4-28 Major and Minor Key Circle of Fifths and Accidentals

Minor Key Scale Forms

When tonality was codified four centuries ago, one of its distinguishing features was the strong gravitational pull between the seventh scale degree and the tonic of the key. The pattern of whole- and half-steps in major keys provides a half step between scale degrees 7 and 1, which creates a strong pull to the tonic. You'll note that in the minor scale, the relationship between scale degrees 7 and 1 is a whole step. To create a stronger pull to the tonic, composers raise the seventh degree of the scale in the minor key when that note goes to scale degree 1. To give the key the flexibility to adjust to different needs, there are three forms of minor scales. The **Natural Minor** scale consists of the notes in the minor key signature. The **Melodic Minor** scale gives the typical notes used when composing minor key melodies. The **Harmonic Minor** scale contains the notes that are most typically used when notes are combined to make **harmony**, or chords.

The best way to think about the various scale forms is to begin with the natural minor and adjust for the melodic and harmonic minor scales.

Below is the key signature for F minor. This is the **natural** form.

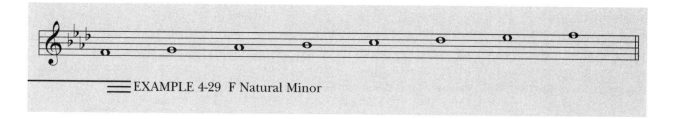

EXAMPLE 4-29 F Natural Minor

Use this as the basis for the two altered scale forms. As the **Melodic Minor** provides the notes most typically used for melodies, there are distinct forms ascending and descending, and you must learn both. When a melody ascends to the tonic through the seventh degree of the scale, that scale degree is raised by one-half step. As that creates a three half-step gap between the sixth and seventh degrees of the scale, the sixth degree is also raised by a half step. So when the melodic notes ascend through scale degrees 6-7-1, scale degrees 6 and 7 are both raised by a half step. If the music is descending from scale degree 1 through scale degrees 7 and 6, these scale degrees are lowered again by half step, which is to say restored to their original notes in the key signature. We will return to this when it is time to compose minor key melodies.

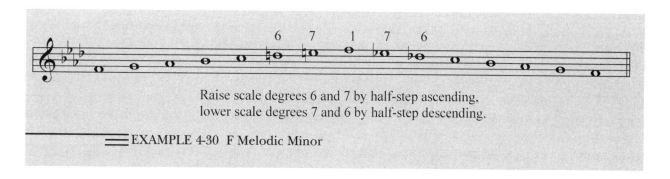

Raise scale degrees 6 and 7 by half-step ascending,
lower scale degrees 7 and 6 by half-step descending.

EXAMPLE 4-30 F Melodic Minor

The **Harmonic Minor** scale serves as the pool of materials typically used for the notes that combine to make chords that accompany melodies. For this scale, we raise the seventh degree by one half step. As these are not scales, per se, and aren't used melodically, the seventh degree is the only one that is altered.

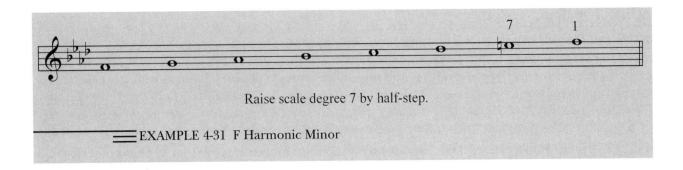

Raise scale degree 7 by half-step.

EXAMPLE 4-31 F Harmonic Minor

Constructing a C# Natural Minor Scale

Here is an opportunity to practice before doing the worksheet at the end of the chapter. Start by putting in the key signature for C# minor. Since there are no alterations in the natural minor scale, just write in the scale starting on "c" sharp. For the melodic minor scale, write the key signature and then write the ascending and descending form of the scale. Raise the sixth and seventh degrees by half-step ascending, and lower them by half step (back to the original pitches) descending. For the harmonic minor, write the "c" sharp minor scale and then raise the seventh degree a half-step. (Note: Whenever you alter a pitch, you must look at the key signature. If the note is flat in the signature, raising it a half-step makes it natural. If it is natural in the key signature, raising it a half-step makes it sharp. If it is sharp in the key signature, raising it a half-step makes it double sharp.)

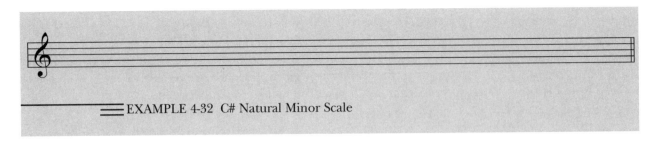

EXAMPLE 4-32 C# Natural Minor Scale

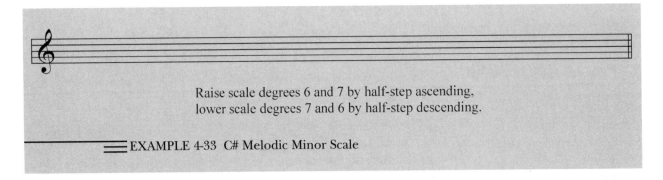

Raise scale degrees 6 and 7 by half-step ascending,
lower scale degrees 7 and 6 by half-step descending.

EXAMPLE 4-33 C# Melodic Minor Scale

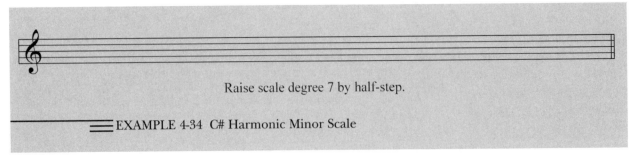

Raise scale degree 7 by half-step.

EXAMPLE 4-34 C# Harmonic Minor Scale

Relative and Parallel Major and Minor

Major and minor keys are said to be related to each other when they share the same key signature or the same tonic note. These keys are compatible, and composers often take advantage of this compatibility by writing sections in the same piece in these related keys.

Relative major and **minor** keys are keys that share the **same key signature but start on different notes.** Keys in the same position on the major key and minor key circle of fifths are relative major and minor to each other. "C" major and "A" minor are relative major and minor, as are "G" major and "e" minor (one sharp). The easiest way to find the relative minor of a major key (or vice versa) is to check the two circles of fifths for the key with the same number of sharps and flats. Another way to find the relative minor from the major is to count up to the sixth scale degree. (Conversely, to find the relative major of a minor key, count up to the third degree of the minor scale.) Another way to find the relative minor from the major is to write the key signature for the major key, write the tonic note, and go down two note names (looking at the key signature). This will give you the relative minor. Going in the other direction, up two note names (looking at the key signature), will give you the relative major from the minor key signature. Another way of saying this is that to find the relative minor from the major, see whether the tonic note of the major is on a space. If it is, go down to the next space and that is the relative minor. If it is on a line, go down to the next line and that will give you the relative minor. If you are trying to find the relative major from the minor, go up to the next space if the minor tonic is on a space and that will give you the relative major. If the minor tonic is on a line, go up to the next line, and that will give you the relative major. All three methods—checking the two circles of fifths, going up or down scale degrees, or looking at the next line or space above or below a note—will yield the same correct results. Find the method that works best for you.

Parallel major and **minor** keys are keys that share the **same tonic note but have different key signatures.** The parallel minor of "C" major is "C" minor, the parallel minor of "Eb" major is "Eb" minor, etc. The simplest way to find the key signature for the parallel major or minor of a given key is by looking at the circle of fifths. Say you are asked to write the parallel minor of "B" major. The parallel minor is "B" minor. Look at the minor key circle of fifths and you will see that "B" minor has two sharps. That is the answer.

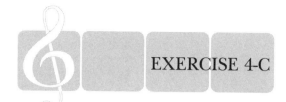

EXERCISE 4-C

Name:_____

Write the key signatures and scales for the Major keys that follow.

Example: B Major   D Major

C Major   F Major

F Major   Eb Major

Ab Major   Bb Major

C# Major   Gb Major

Db Major   A Major

G Major   F# Major

Cb Major   G Major

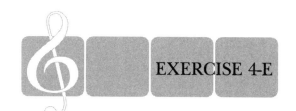

EXERCISE 4-E

Name: _____

Write the key signature and one tonic note for each of the Major keys below.

Example: E Major   G Major   F Major

C Major   B Major   Ab Major

F# Major   D Major   Eb Major

Cb Major   C# Major   Bb Major

A Major   F# Major   Db Major

E Major   F Major   F# Major

Ab Major   D Major   B Major

Gb Major   Bb Major   A Major

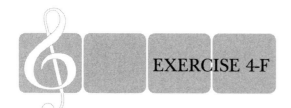

EXERCISE 4-F

Name: _____

Without using a key signature, write the **natural minor scales** for the following keys. Write the key names under the scales.

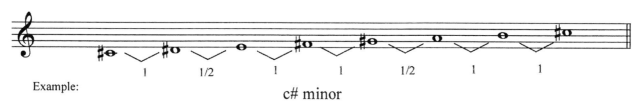

Example:

c# minor

B minor

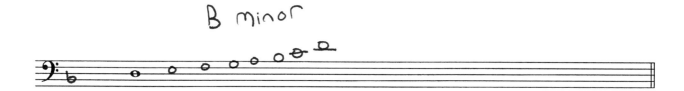

d Minor

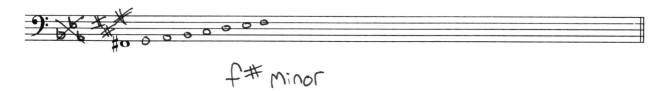

f# Minor

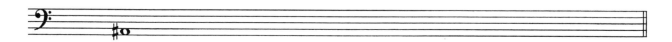

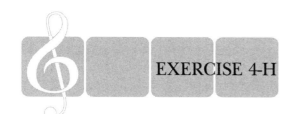

EXERCISE 4-H

Name: _____

Write the key names for the following minor key signatures and supply the tonic.

Example: bb minor

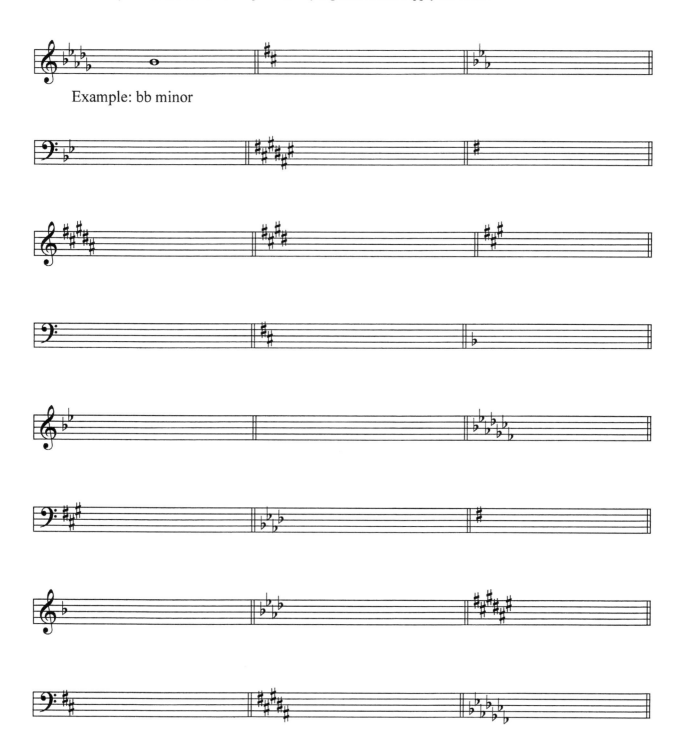

EXERCISE 4-I

Name: _____

Write the key signature and one tonic note for each of the minor keys below.

Example: c# minor　　　　　e minor　　　　　f minor

g minor　　　　　b minor　　　　　ab minor

f# minor　　　　　d minor　　　　　d# minor

eb minor　　　　　c# minor　　　　　bb minor

a minor　　　　　f# minor　　　　　g# minor

e minor　　　　　d# minor　　　　　f minor

ab minor　　　　　bb minor　　　　　b minor

g# minor　　　　　d minor　　　　　a minor

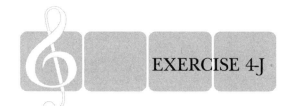

EXERCISE 4-J

Name: _____

Write the scale forms for the following minor keys. For the natural and harmonic minor, only write the ascending scale form.

For the melodic minor, write the ascending <u>and</u> descending scale forms.

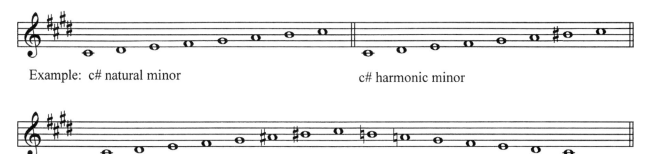

Example: c# natural minor   c# harmonic minor

c# melodic minor

g natural minor   g harmonic minor

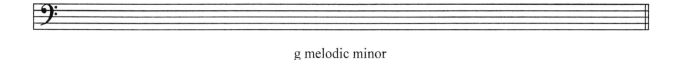

g melodic minor

f# natural minor   f# harmonic minor

f# melodic minor

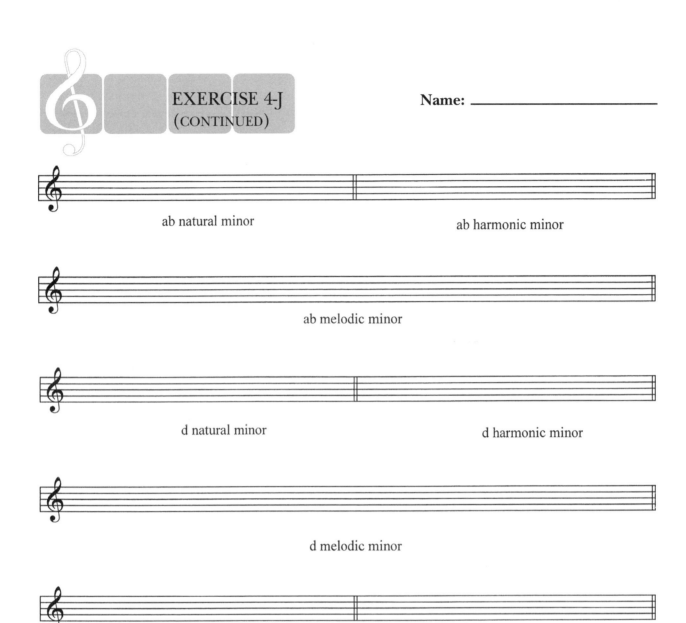

ab natural minor

ab harmonic minor

ab melodic minor

d natural minor

d harmonic minor

d melodic minor

e natural minor

e harmonic minor

e melodic minor

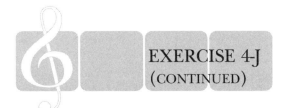

Name: _____

a natural minor   a harmonic minor

a melodic minor

EXERCISE 4-K

Name: _____

For the first key given, write the key signature, the key name, and the ascending scale form, making alterations in the minor scales if called for.

For the second key, write the key name and the scale, making alterations if necessary.

For the natural and harmonic minor, you need only write the ascending scale. For the melodic minor, write the ascending and descending forms of the scale.

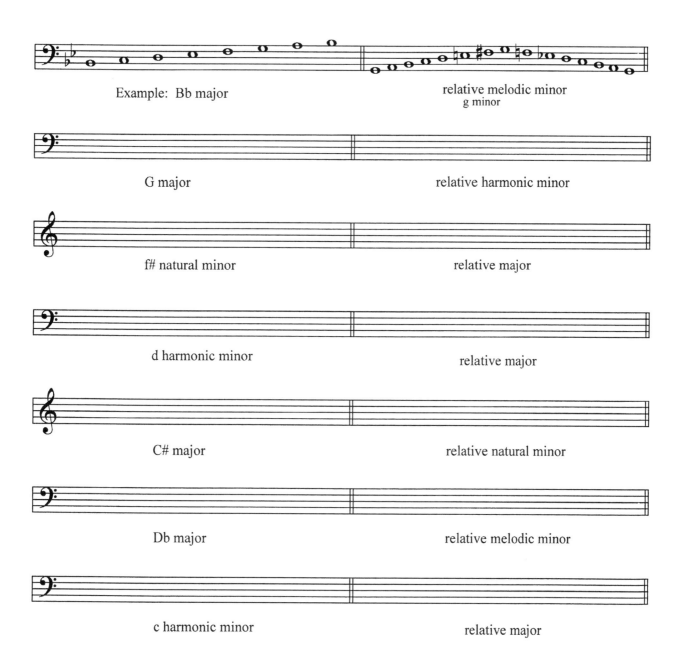

Example: Bb major   relative melodic minor
g minor

G major   relative harmonic minor

f# natural minor   relative major

d harmonic minor   relative major

C# major   relative natural minor

Db major   relative melodic minor

c harmonic minor   relative major

EXERCISE 4-K
(CONTINUED)

Name: _____

        E major   relative harmonic minor

EXERCISE 4-L

Name: _____

For the first key given, write the key signature, the key name, and the ascending scale form, making alterations in the minor scales if called for.

For the second key, write the key name and the scale, making alterations if necessary.

For the natural and harmonic minor, you need only write the ascending scale. For the melodic minor, write the ascending and descending forms of the scale.

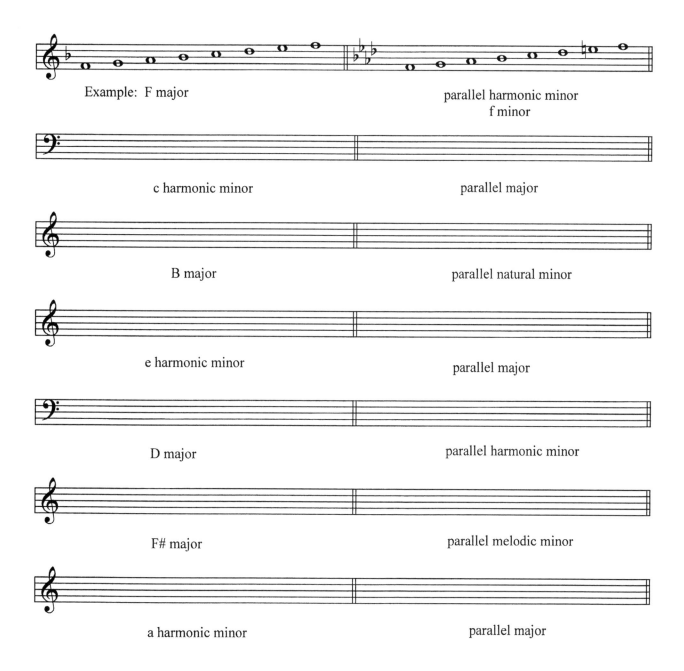

Example: F major

parallel harmonic minor
f minor

c harmonic minor

parallel major

B major

parallel natural minor

e harmonic minor

parallel major

D major

parallel harmonic minor

F# major

parallel melodic minor

a harmonic minor

parallel major

EXERCISE 4-L
(CONTINUED)

Name: _____

Eb major   parallel melodic minor

Intervals

The distance between any two notes is called an **interval**, and this describes the relationship between any two notes whether they are played consecutively or simultaneously. When two notes are played consecutively, we call the sound a **melodic interval.** When played simultaneously, we call the sound a **harmonic interval.** Naming intervals is a useful way to describe the sound of the relationship between any two notes as each interval has a different sonority. It is also an important building block in learning how to construct melodies and chords. The knowledge we gain in this chapter will be essential when we learn how to build chords in Chapter 8.

Intervals are measured and described in terms of distance and quality. Distance is easy to calculate. For simple intervals (those going no higher than eight scale note names), we use numbers 1 through 8 to describe the distance between any two notes up to an octave. Looking at any two notes, we begin with the bottom note, count that as 1, and count up consecutive lines and spaces, or note names, until we land on the second note. That figure is the distance between the two notes. In Example 5-1a below, we count up from "e" to "b," counting "e" as 1. "F" is 2, "g" is 3, "a" is 4, and "b" is 5. The distance between the two intervals is a fifth, expressed as a numeral. In b), we count "c#" as 1, "d" as 2, "e" as 3, "f" as 4, "g" as 5, "a" as 6, and "b" as 7. We call the interval a seventh, and represent it with a numeral. In example c), we call "bb" 1, "c" 2, and "d" 3, labeling the interval a third and representing it as a number.

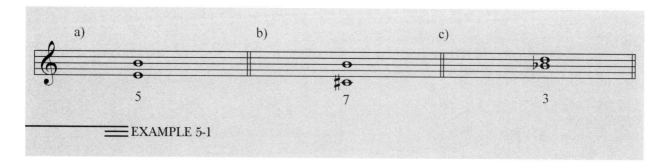

EXAMPLE 5-1

Note in the following example that melodic intervals are also expressed the same way. In example a) below, we count up from "c" to "a," counting "c" as 1. "D" is 2, "e" is 3, "f" is 4, "g" is 5, and "a" is 6. We call that interval a sixth. We follow the same procedure for examples b) and c). "Ab" to "db" in example b), consists of four note names ("a," "b," "c," and "d,") so it is a fourth. In example c), c# to d# involves only two note names, so it is a second.

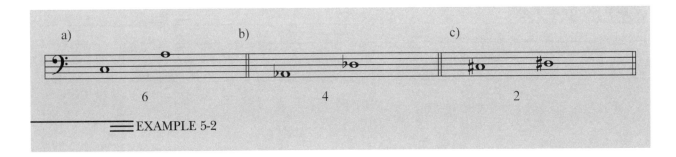

EXAMPLE 5-2

Intervals also have a **quality** designation. Every interval has two components, a quality and numeral designation. There are five quality designations. They are **diminished, minor, major, perfect**, and **augmented.** Some of these quality designations only go with certain intervals. The chart below describes what quality designations go with what intervals. The qualities we use for each group of intervals is listed below the intervals. Note that intervals of a unison (1), fourth (4), fifth (5), and octave (8) get the quality designators **diminished, perfect**, and **augmented**, whereas the intervals of the second (2), third (3), sixth (6), and seventh (7) don't use the term "perfect" but add the qualities "major" and "minor." So seconds, thirds, sixths, and sevenths are described as **diminished, minor, major**, and **augmented.** You will need to memorize the chart below. The abbreviations we use for qualities are as follows: diminished=d; minor=m; major=M; augmented=A. When we refer to a d5, we mean a diminished fifth; a P5 is a perfect fifth; m7 is a minor seventh; M3 is a major third, and so on.

<table>
<tr><td>Perfect Intervals</td><td>Major/Minor Intervals</td></tr>
<tr><td>1, 4, 5, 8</td><td>2, 3, 6, 7</td></tr>
<tr><td>Quality names: diminished, perfect, augmented</td><td>diminished, minor, major, augmented</td></tr>
</table>

Note that intervals of a unison, fourth, fifth, and octave are never labeled "major" or "minor," while intervals of second, third, sixth, and seventh, are never labeled "perfect."

As we move from left to right in our quality designators, the intervals get larger. In the following group of intervals for 1, 4, 5, and 8, each successive term to the right makes the interval a half step bigger. From c to gb is a diminished fifth (six half-steps). From c to g is a perfect fifth (seven half-steps). From c to g# is an augmented interval (eight half-steps). In the second example, note again that the intervals get wider as we go from left to right. C to ebb (double flat) is a diminished third (two half-steps), c to eb is a minor third (three half-steps), c to e is a major third (four half-steps), and c to e# is an augmented third (five half-steps).

As you read from left to right in the chart below, the interval expands by one-half step and one numerical interval is given as an example.

Perfect Intervals (1, 4, 5, 8)			Major/Minor Intervals (2, 3, 6, 7)			
Diminished	Perfect	Augmented	Diminished	Minor	Major	Augmented
c-gb	c-g	c-g#	c-ebb	c-eb	c-e	c-e#
6-1/2 steps	7-1/2 steps	8-1/2 steps	2-1/2 steps	3-1/2 steps	4-1/2 steps	5-1/2 steps

EXAMPLE 5-3

The Scale Method

There are two methods for determining intervals, and you should try both and use the one that works for you. The first method is to learn all the intervals associated with the major scale. This will teach you one of each of the eight intervals, and you can modify those intervals by using the chart in Example 5-3 to find other intervals. Note below that all of the intervals from tonic to the successive scale degrees are either major (2nds, 3rds, 6ths, and 7ths) or perfect (4ths, 5ths, and 8ths, or octaves).

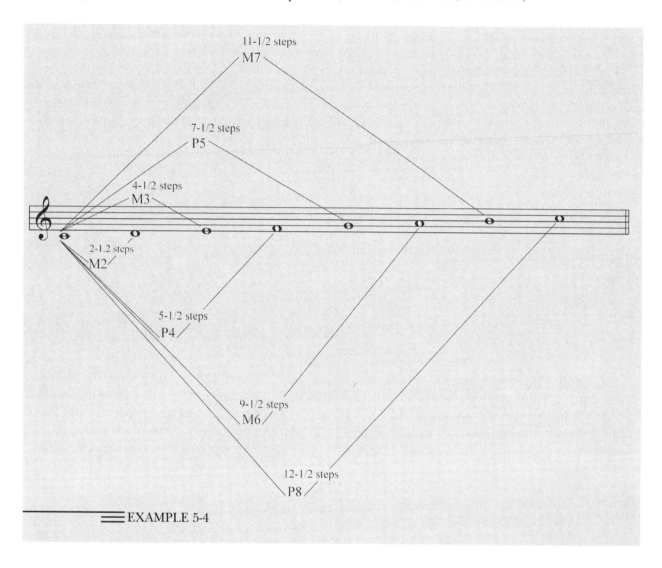

EXAMPLE 5-4

Looking at "c" as the bottom note of any interval pair, we can find or construct the following intervals by simply using scale steps of the "c" major scale. The pattern of intervals is created in the example below and is consistent for all major scales.

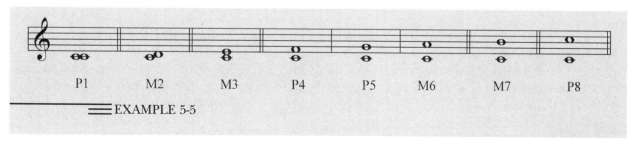

EXAMPLE 5-5

Using this method, you would assume that every bottom note of your two-note (or **dyad**) pair is the tonic note of a major scale. Then if you were asked to construct a M2, from "e," for example, you would count up to the second note of the "E" Major scale, "f#", and that would give you the answer. If you were asked to write a minor 2nd, you would count up to the second degree of the "E" Major scale, "f#", and look at your chart in 5-3. Note that when you want to make a major interval into a minor one, you reduce the interval by a half step. Reducing the "f#" by a half step makes it "f" natural; the interval from "e" to "f" is a minor second. Similarly, if asked to produce an augmented 2nd starting on "e," you would first find the interval you know. "E" to "f#" is a M2. To increase the interval to an A2, look at the chart. An A2 is one-half step larger than a M2, so you would make the "f#" an "f" double sharp. Following this procedure, you could derive any interval from the seven that you know.

Let's practice one example using this method. Write an A6 (augmented sixth) above the given note. You are given an "f" and asked to construct an A6 above the note. Imagine an "F" Major scale and count up to the sixth degree, which is "d" (Example 5-5b). You know that in a major key, the sixth degree is major (see Example 5-4). "F" to "d" is a major sixth. To make a major interval into an augmented one, you must increase its size by one half step. The d natural becomes a "d#" (see Example 5c).

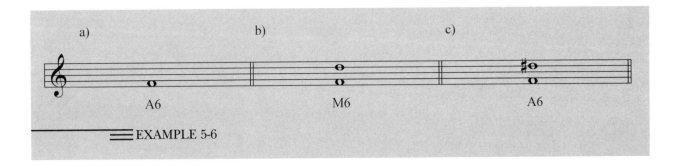

EXAMPLE 5-6

Once you have found the M6, it is easy to alter the interval to reflect other qualities by referring to the chart in Example 5-3. If you were asked to write a minor sixth, you would reduce the M6 by a half step, lowering the "d" natural to "db" (see Example 5-7b); if you wanted to construct a d6, you would make the interval two half steps smaller than a M6 (Example 5-7c). Example 5-7 shows the four different possibilities for the interval of a sixth, the latter three possible to derive once you know the M6.

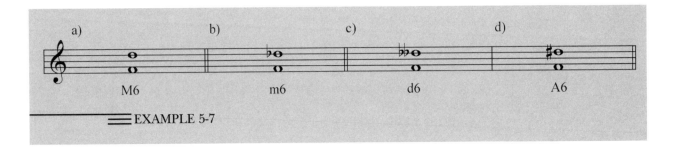

EXAMPLE 5-7

When asked to label an interval, the procedure is the same. Imagine that the bottom note is the tonic and count it as 1, and continue counting to the second note. That is the interval number. Now figure out whether the note given above the "tonic" is a member of the major scale beginning on that tonic note. If it is, then you already have the answer. For example, if the bottom note is "eb," and the note above it is "bb," then you count up from "eb" to "bb" and get the number 5 (refer to Example 5-8). You know from the chart in Example 5-4 that the fifth degree of any major scale is a P5 (perfect fifth). "Bb" IS the fifth degree of the "Eb" major scale, so you know that that interval is a P5. But what if the note was "b" natural? Since you know that "bb" is a P5, you only need to refer to the chart in Example 5-3 to know that an interval that is a half step above a P5 is an A5 (augmented fifth). Similarly, if the note was a "b" double flat, you would also begin with what you know, that a "bb" would make a P5 above "eb." Refer again to the chart in Example 5-3 and you'll observe that an interval that is a half step smaller than any perfect interval makes it a diminished interval. Therefore, the interval from "eb" to "b" double flat is a d5 (diminished fifth). With practice, you will become adept at figuring out the intervals.

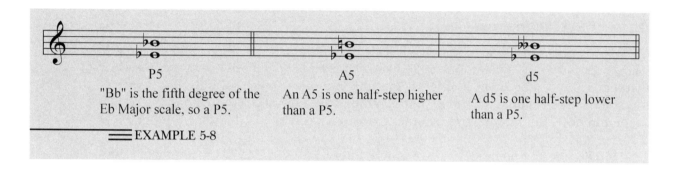

P5

"Bb" is the fifth degree of the Eb Major scale, so a P5.

A5

An A5 is one half-step higher than a P5.

d5

A d5 is one half-step lower than a P5.

EXAMPLE 5-8

Try this method on your own, or with the help of your teacher. In Example 5-9, construct the intervals requested. The first one is given. In Example 5-10, name the intervals. The first answer is given. Note in Example 5-9 that examples (b), (c), and (d) only require that you find the major scale degrees of each interval since the intervals asked for are consistent with those of the major scale. In examples (e) and (f), you are asked to construct diminished and augmented intervals, which do not exist naturally in the major scale from the tonic note to other scale degrees. In example (e), find the note that is the P5 (perfect fifth) of a "d" major scale (the fifth scale degree), and alter that note to make it diminished by adding the accidental that makes it a half step smaller. In example (f), find the note that is a M6 (major sixth) above the given note and make it augmented by using an accidental to raise it by a half step.

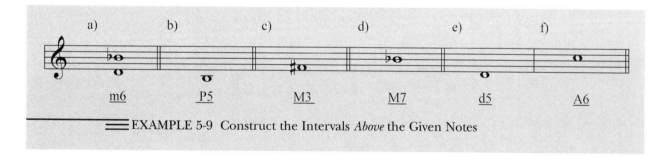

a)	b)	c)	d)	e)	f)
m6	P5	M3	M7	d5	A6

EXAMPLE 5-9 Construct the Intervals *Above* the Given Notes

As you do the exercises in Example 5-10, note that in examples (a), (b), (c), and (d), the top note is a member of the scale of the bottom note. This is not the case in examples (e), and (f). Once you figure out what degree of the scale the top note would be, you can figure out what the actual given pitch is in relation to the scale pitch by referring to the chart in Example 5-3.

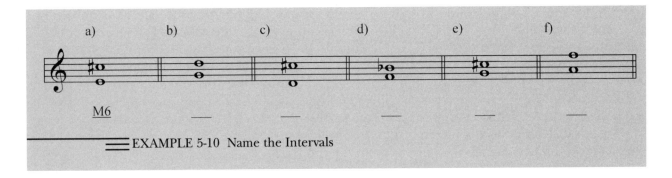

EXAMPLE 5-10 Name the Intervals

Memorizing the Interval Chart

Comparing pitches to those of the major scale to determine intervals is reliable, and reinforcing scale degrees helps a student understand keys, an essential component of tonal music. But the method is also cumbersome, as one has to think in terms of scales to derive every interval. It is also misleading, as it assumes that every bottom note of an interval is a tonic note of a scale in relation to the top note. But most intervals in music do not exist between the tonic note of the key and another note.

There is another method for determining intervals. It is somewhat mathematical and counter-intuitive to the way most musicians think about intervals. But it is reliable, simple, and will give the student of music theory much-needed practice in determining intervals fairly quickly. Eventually, musicians come to know what intervals are without counting or "figuring."

The chart in Example 5-11 gives the number of half and whole steps between the most important intervals from P1 to P8. For example, there are two half steps in a major second, 7 half steps in a P5, and so on. To save you time, you might just memorize the number of half (or whole) steps for one of each interval between a M2 and M7 (given in bold print). Then if you are asked to identify an interval or construct an interval other than the ones you've memorized, just use the chart in Example 5-3 to make the adjustment.

	Interval Chart	
Interval	Distance	
	1/2 Steps	whole steps
P1	0	0
m2	1	1/2
M2	**2**	**1**
m3	3	1 1/2
M3	**4**	**2**
P4	**5**	**2 1/2**
A4/d5	6	3
P5	**7**	**3 1/2**
m6	8	4
M6	**9**	**4 1/2**
m7	10	5
M7	**11**	**5 1/2**
P8	12	6

EXAMPLE 5-11

Let's try this method. Say you are asked to **construct** a perfect fifth above the note "f#" (Example 5-12). First count up starting with 1 on "f#." "C" is the fifth note name above "f#." Now count the number of half steps between "f#" and "c." Since these are intervals, you count 1 on "g," 2 on "g#," 3 on "a," and so on until you reach "c." There are six half steps between "f#" and "c." As you see from the chart above, and as you'll know when you memorize one of each interval, there are seven half-steps in a perfect fifth. You must increase the size of the interval from six to seven half steps by raising "c" one half-step to "c#." That gives you seven half steps, or a perfect fifth.

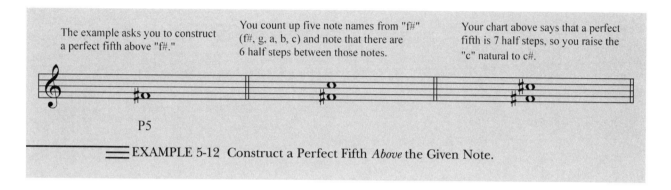

The example asks you to construct a perfect fifth above "f#."

You count up five note names from "f#" (f#, g, a, b, c) and note that there are 6 half steps between those notes.

Your chart above says that a perfect fifth is 7 half steps, so you raise the "c" natural to c#.

P5

EXAMPLE 5-12 Construct a Perfect Fifth *Above* the Given Note.

If you are asked to **name** an interval, the method is the same. You write the interval example you've memorized and then relate it to the interval you are given. For example, say you are given the notes "f" and "d" to name (see Example 5-13). "F" to "d" is a 6 ("f," "g," "a," "b," "c," "d"). You look at your chart or memorize that there are nine half-steps in a M6. You count the half steps from "f" to "d" ("f" to "f#" is 1, "f#" to "g" is 2, and so on) and discover that there are nine half steps between "f" and "d." Nine half steps between notes a sixth apart IS a M6, so that's your answer. What if the interval you are asked to identify is from "f" to "db"? Since you know that "f" to "d" is a M6 (major sixth), an interval that is a half step smaller is a m6 (minor sixth). If the notes are "f" to "d" double flat, then the interval is a d6 (diminished sixth), two half steps smaller than a M6. If the interval is "f" to "d#," then the interval would be labeled an A6 (augmented sixth) because it is a half step bigger than a M6.

Example 5-13 shows the interval you know, M6, nine half steps. The other intervals can be gleaned if you have memorized that one interval for a sixth. Until you memorize the number of half steps in one of each of the intervals from M2 to M7 and the order of interval qualities, you should refer to the charts in Examples 5-3 and 5-11. You will get better, and the procedure will become clearer, with practice.

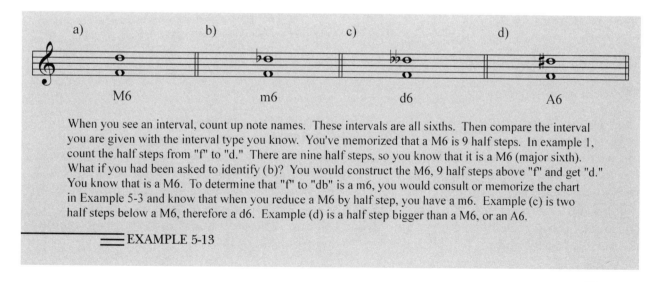

a)   b)   c)   d)

M6   m6   d6   A6

When you see an interval, count up note names. These intervals are all sixths. Then compare the interval you are given with the interval type you know. You've memorized that a M6 is 9 half steps. In example 1, count the half steps from "f" to "d." There are nine half steps, so you know that it is a M6 (major sixth). What if you had been asked to identify (b)? You would construct the M6, 9 half steps above "f" and get "d." You know that is a M6. To determine that "f" to "db" is a m6, you would consult or memorize the chart in Example 5-3 and know that when you reduce a M6 by half step, you have a m6. Example (c) is two half steps below a M6, therefore a d6. Example (d) is a half step bigger than a M6, or an A6.

EXAMPLE 5-13

Try this method on your own, or with the help of your teacher. In Example 5-12, construct the intervals requested. The first one is given. In Example 5-13, name the intervals. The first answer is given. In some cases, the intervals will be the ones you memorized. In others, you will have to extrapolate from the intervals you know from the chart (Example 5-11) to get the ones you are asked for.

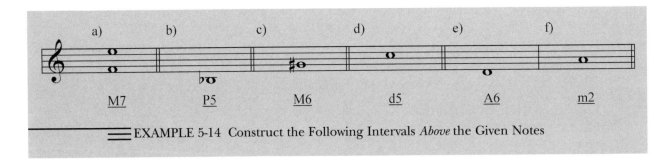

EXAMPLE 5-14 Construct the Following Intervals *Above* the Given Notes

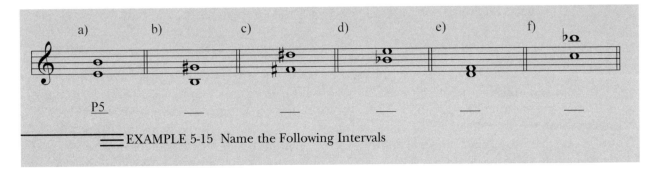

EXAMPLE 5-15 Name the Following Intervals

In the case of intervals of an eighth, remember that a P8 (an octave) is the same note as the bottom note, reproduced in the next higher register. As you can see in Example 5-16, there are two "c#'s" in consecutive octaves. To find the A8, raise the top note one half-step; to find the d8, lower the top note one half-step.

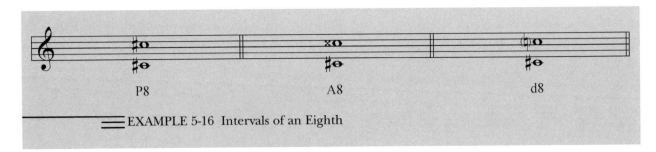

EXAMPLE 5-16 Intervals of an Eighth

A useful shortcut for students learning about intervals is that perfect fourths and perfect fifths are very consistent in their construction. In the perfect fourth, if the bottom note is natural, the top note will be also. If the bottom note is flat, the top note will be flat as well. If the bottom note is sharp, the top note will be sharp as well. The exceptions are from the notes "f" to "bb" and "f#" to "b," which are perfect fourths. Similarly, with perfect fifths, natural notes go with natural notes, flat notes go with flat notes, and sharp notes go with sharp notes. The exceptions are "bb" to "f" and "b" to "f#." If you remember the exceptions, you will have an easier time constructing and identifying perfect fourths and perfect fifths.

Inversions

Another shortcut in constructing or identifying intervals is using **inversions.** When you **invert** an interval, you simply move the bottom note up an octave or the top note down an octave so that the notes's relationship to each other is turned upside down. In Example 5-17a the "c" is inverted so that it is closer to the "a." In Example 5-17b, the "f" is inverted so that it is closer to the "g." In 5-17c, the "eb" is inverted so that it is closer to, and above, the "d."

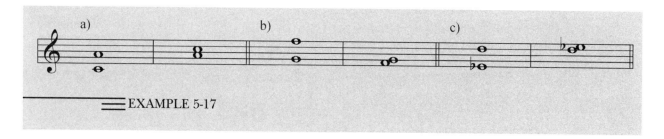

EXAMPLE 5-17

There is a formula governing inversions, as follows:

Minor intervals invert to major intervals (and vice versa).
Perfect intervals invert to perfect intervals (and vice versa)
Diminished intervals invert to augmented intervals (and vice versa).

Inverted intervals together also add up to a ninth (9). When you invert a second, it becomes a seventh (and vice versa). Inverted thirds become sixths, and inverted fourths become fifths. If you look at Example 5-18, you'll see the third in example (a) becomes a sixth, the seventh in (b) becomes a second, and in (c), the fifth becomes a fourth. These integers all add up to 9.

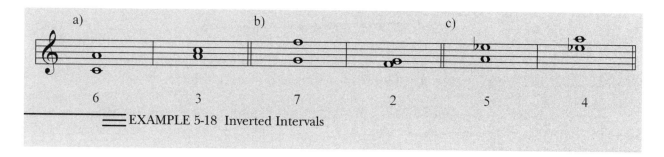

EXAMPLE 5-18 Inverted Intervals

You will further notice that in Example 15-19, the inversion quality and numerals is as discussed above: minor and major intervals invert to each other, perfect intervals invert to each other, and diminished and augmented intervals invert to each other. In addition, subtract the first interval from nine and you will get the other interval. In the three examples, the M6 inverts to a m3 in (a); the m7 inverts to a M2 in (b); and the d5 inverts to an A4 in (c).

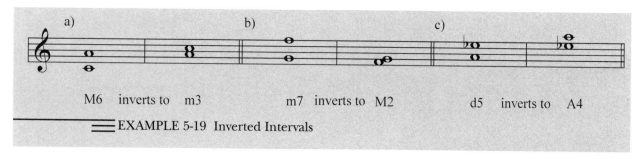

M6   inverts to   m3   m7   inverts to   M2   d5   inverts to   A4

EXAMPLE 5-19 Inverted Intervals

This will be helpful if you want to write a large interval or name it. For example, if you want to write a large interval, you need only find the inversion and then reverse the order of the notes. In other words, in Example 5-20, you are asked to construct a M7 above "d." If you construct its inversion and then move the bottom note up an octave, you will find the M7. The inversion of a M7 will be a m2 (major intervals invert to minor ones, and seven subtracted from nine equals two, or a second (2)). That means that if you construct a m2 and invert it, you will have a M7. In the example below, in (a) we have the note and the instruction to write a M7. In (b), we write its inversion, a m2. In, (c), we invert the bottom note, which forms the M7.

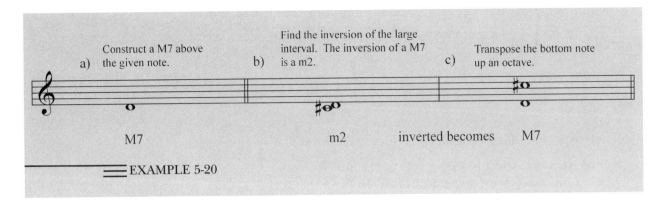

EXAMPLE 5-20

Constructing Intervals Below a Note

Sometimes you'll want to write an interval below a note. When doing so, the procedure is the same as writing above a note, except that you never alter the given note. When writing a note *below* another note, count down from the given note, counting it as one, until you reach the note interval number you are looking for. Then use your chart in Example 5-11 to adjust the quality.

In Example 5-21, you are asked to write an A6 below the given note "e." First count to six down the staff starting on "e." A sixth below is g (see (a) below). Count the number of half steps between "e" and "g." The answer is nine. You know from your chart in Example 5-11 or have already memorized that nine half steps equals a major sixth. Now look at the chart in Example 5-3. To make a major interval a half step larger, you have to widen the interval by one half step. But since you cannot alter the top note, you must expand the interval using the bottom note. You will therefore **lower** the bottom note by a half step, from "g" to "gb" (example (b) below), in order to make the interval ten half steps rather than nine.

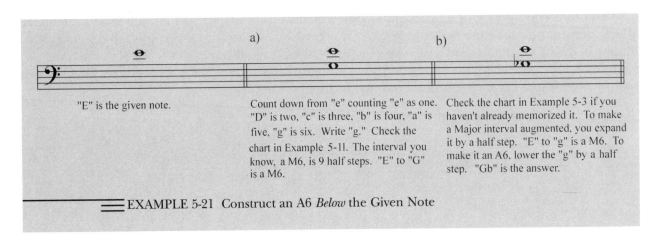

"E" is the given note.

Count down from "e" counting "e" as one. "D" is two, "c" is three, "b" is four, "a" is five, "g" is six. Write "g." Check the chart in Example 5-11. The interval you know, a M6, is 9 half steps. "E" to "G" is a M6.

Check the chart in Example 5-3 if you haven't already memorized it. To make a Major interval augmented, you expand it by a half step. "E" to "g" is a M6. To make it an A6, lower the "g" by a half step. "Gb" is the answer.

EXAMPLE 5-21 Construct an A6 *Below* the Given Note

Practice constructing intervals *below* a given note in Example 5-22. The first answer is given.

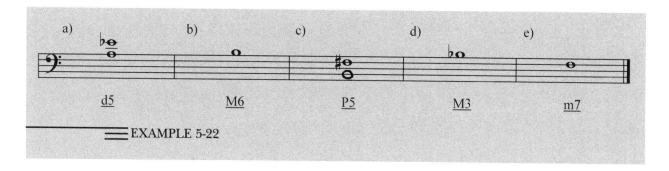

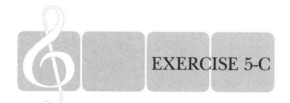

EXERCISE 5-C

Name: _____

Construct the following intervals <u>below</u> the given notes.

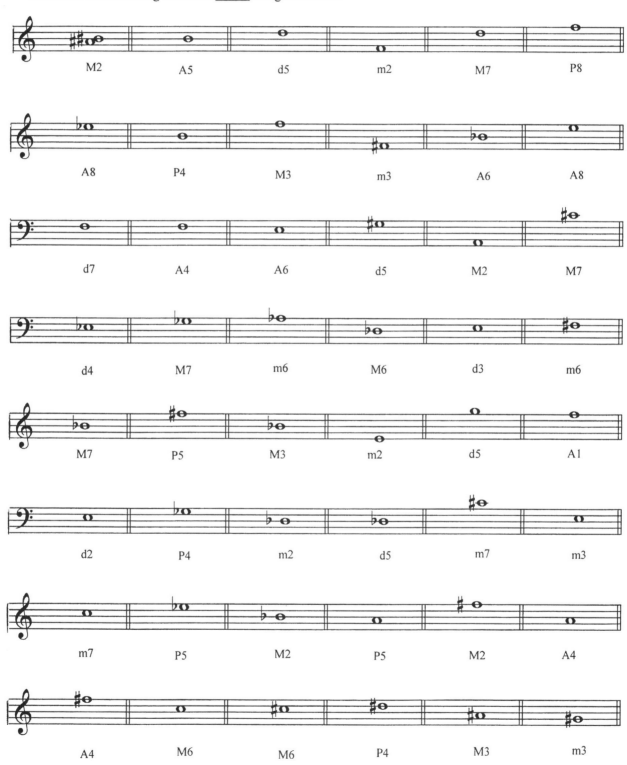

Note: When notes are a second apart, the bottom note goes to the left of the top note.
When acidentials are involved, the bottom accidential goes to the left of the top note accidental.

99

Motives and Themes Writing Major Key Melodies

CHAPTER 6

MOTIVES AND THEMES

We have seen in previous chapters that there are many consistencies in the language of music. The major scale always has the same intervallic pattern, the circle of fifths adds one sharp as it rises by perfect fifths, there are always five half steps in a perfect fourth, and so on. In this chapter, we are introduced to a more subjective element of music, the creation of melody. A **melody** is a linear arrangement of notes and rhythms, generally created to produce a memorable effect. Another word for melody is "tune," while the Classical music term is **theme.** A melody becomes a theme when it figures prominently in a piece of music. Themes are often made up of smaller units of melodic material called **motives.** To be considered a motive, a unit of material must be significantly repeated throughout a piece or a movement (a self-contained section) of a piece. Motives are identified by their intervallic and rhythmic components. Throughout the history of Western music, composers have used motives and themes and found ingenious ways of developing and varying them. The use of themes and motives helps create coherence in music. Varying motives and themes creates a sense of spontaneity, freshness, and growth, while still retaining recognizable elements that a knowledgeable listener enjoys following.

Perhaps the most famous motive in Western music is the one that begins the *Symphony No. 5 in C Minor* by Ludwig van Beethoven (1770–1827). The motive is a mere four notes, and three of them are the same. The symphony begins with this motive, unaccompanied.

EXAMPLE 6-1 Opening, Beethoven *Symphony No. 5*

The symbol below the "eb" in measure 2 is called a "fermata," which tells the players to hold the note until the conductor gestures to stop. This little motive becomes an essential building block not only of the first movement of the four-movement symphony, but figures prominently in the third and fourth movements as well.

One aspect of Beethoven's compositional brilliance was his ability to create magnificent structures of great substance out of the most seemingly simple shreds of motivic material. After the initial presentation of the four-note motive reproduced in Example 6-1, he builds a compelling theme out of successive iterations of that simple motive, bracketed below.

EXAMPLE 6-2 First theme, Beethoven *Symphony No. 5*, movement 1

As you can see, Beethoven uses this motive, verbatim or varied, nine times in the construction of the symphony's first theme (excluding the accompaniment, where it also occurs). This motive occurs hundreds of times throughout the first movement, developing a mighty structure out of a very simple idea. Threaded through the symphony, the motive helps Beethoven create coherence through repetition and variety through elaboration, and the listener is invited to follow the change and growth of a recognizable musical idea.

Another example of the extensive use of a motive occurs in the second of a set of pieces composed by Johann Sebastian Bach (1685–1750) called The Well-Tempered Clavier, Book 1 ("clavier" is a German word for keyboard), which contains 24 Preludes and Fugues. Each pair of preludes and fugues is written in a different key, twelve in major and twelve in minor, covering every key of the chromatic scale. In the Fugue in C Minor, a single motive dominates the piece (although there are other motives as well). Like the opening of Beethoven's *Symphony No. 5*, Bach's motive is short, only five notes. Like Beethoven also, Bach uses this motive (bracketed below) as a building block to create a theme (called a **subject** in a fugue).

EXAMPLE 6-3 Opening subject from J.S. Bach's Fugue in C Minor, from Well-Tempered Clavier, Book 1

Notice the rhythm of the opening motive: two sixteenth notes followed by three eighth notes. This same rhythmic idea is repeated twice. A repetitive rhythmic idea is called a **figure.** Notice how Bach creates consistency in his melody through the repetition of that five-note rhythmic figure. The three successive iterations of the rhythmic figure have three different melodic profiles. Bach creates motivic variety, but knits the whole together through the use of a consistent rhythmic shape. Much of the composition is built on this motive. The literal five-note motive that starts the piece occurs several times (sometimes stated in different keys), while the five-note rhythmic figure occurs even more often throughout the piece. Sometimes the opening motive or figure occurs in full statements of the subject, sometimes it is found in passages that string together successive statements of the five-note motive. As for the five-note rhythmic figure attached to the opening motivic idea—two sixteenth notes followed by three eighth notes—this figure is heard in all but two measures of this composition. Bach saturates the piece with this rhythmic figure, while constantly varying the pitches to maintain interest.

Writing a Major Key Melody

Every composer has a different approach to the creation of melodies. Among composers of tonal music (music in a key), Bach's, Mozart's, Beethoven's, Schubert's, Brahms's, and Mahler's melodies have their own personalities. So do those of composers like Gershwin, Cole Porter, Paul McCartney, and John Lennon. There is no formula for creating a melody like there is for constructing a major scale or identifying a minor sixth, which is why the melodies of composers are so refreshingly varied and unique. But for the student learning music theory, following a certain set of instructions will produce effective results. Our assignment by the end of the chapter is to write an eight-measure melody in a major key.

Why an eight-measure melody? One of the helpful organizational principles in composing is the creation of symmetrical **phrases,** that is, self-contained melodic lines that are the same length and are clearly related to each other.

Play the following example on the piano.

EXAMPLE 6-4 Major Key Melody

First, you know from the key signature—one sharp—that the melody is either in G major or E minor. How do we distinguish the relative major and minor keys from each other? One way is to look at the note on which the melody ends. It is a "g." Melodies often end on the tonic note of the scale, as the gravitational pull of tonality makes the tonic the most "resolved" and stable note of the scale. Another hint as to the key is the absence of any accidentals. As we saw in Chapter 4, the minor key requires the raising of the seventh scale degree to create a leading tone, that is, a tone only a half-step from tonic that creates a strong gravitational pull back to tonic. Although it is possible to avoid writing a minor key melody without including scale degree 7, that note frequently does appear, and will generally be raised when it goes to the tonic (1) of the scale. It will also certainly be seen in the accompaniment to a melody if one exists. The absence of accidentals in a passage or melody would indicate that the key is major. Most importantly, if you play through it, you will discover that it *sounds* major, and the arrival on the tonic pitch at the end cements that impression.

Creating Coherent Phrases

Looking further at the melody, we observe that it is eight measures long. Those eight measures can be further subdivided into two four-measure units or phrases. One element that makes the division into two phrases clear is the fact that measure 5, the beginning of the second four-measure phrase, repeats the first measure. "Beginning" again helps demarcate this four-measure phrase from the previous one. The melody's only dotted rhythm (dotted quarter followed by a dotted eighth note) is found in measures 1 and 5, further solidifying the identity of each of these measures as the beginning of a phrase. You'll also notice that in addition to the fifth measure repeating the first, measures 5–7 also refer to the pitches used in measures 1–3. Measures 2 and 6 begin with the note "c," and measures 3 and 7 begin with "e." Measures 4 and 8 have a different melodic contour but are similar rhythmically, in that both begin with four eighth notes.

A combination of melodic and rhythmic elements creates a sense of coherence in the construction of two similar four-measure phrases. But note that the two phrases are not exactly the same. Composers often vary their musical ideas in an attempt to avoid monotony and create drama. In this particular melody, measures 3–4 and 7–8 are recognizably related to each other, but are different in their details. Measure eight has the melody's only half note, an appropriate lengthening of duration consistent with the winding down of the melody. But it is measures 2 and 6 that are the most different. The highest note in measure 2 is the "d" on the upbeat (the second eighth note) of beat 2. In measure 6, the music climbs all the way up to "g," the highest note of the piece. This is the registral high point of the melody, and it is "saved" for the final phrase as an arrival point. It is also satisfying because in addition to being the highest note of the melody, it is also the tonic of the key.

On a more subtle, "behind the scenes" level, is the skeletal structure of the music line underpinning the melody in measures 3–4 and 7–8. Look at the circled notes in Example 6-5. You'll notice that there is a descending scale, "e" down to "a" in measures 3–4. But the scale stops on "a," which is the second degree of the scale. Because the melody pauses on scale degree 2, there is no sense of finality. "G" is the note of finality, as it is the tonic of the key. Notice in measures 7–8 that there is also a descending scale that starts on "e." The notes go from "e" down to "d" to "c" to "b," to "a," but this time, as we come to the end of the melody, descends further to "g." This is the tonic of the key and landing on "g" creates a sense of finality and closure that is appropriate to the ending. The scale anchoring measures 3–4 pauses on "a." The scale anchoring measures 7–8 repeat the same scale but continues down to "g," creating a sense of resolution.

EXAMPLE 6-5 Major Key Melody

You might notice other aspects of the melody that help to organize it and make it coherent. Each four-measure phrase can be further subdivided into two two-measure phrases, the second commenting on the first. The pool of rhythmic materials is restricted to only four note values: the dotted quarter, quarter, eighth, and half note, and the half note is used only once to reinforce the sense of arrival and rest at the end of the piece. You will also notice that the majority of the intervals, 23 of 41, are major and minor seconds. The largest interval is a minor 6 and that only occurs one time. Most melodies, especially those intended to be sung, contain many seconds. This creates a smooth, singable line. Leaps create variety, drama, and a degree of expressivity. Finally, you'll notice that there is a persistent motive in our model melody, Example 6-5. This motive ascends by step and descends by a leap of a third. This motive is bracketed in measures 2, 3, 4, and 7 and occurs six times in the space of eight measures. An intervalically expanded version, a leap up a minor third and down a perfect fourth, occurs in measure 1 and in the repeat of that melody in measure 5. In all, there are eight occurrences of this basic figure, which helps to give the melody a great deal of consistency.

Suggestions for Writing a Major Key Melody

Prior to composing your melody, look at the following set of principles extrapolated from the discussion above. Although there is no formula for writing good melodies, and many melodies do not do everything suggested below, following the suggestions will guide you in creating a convincing melody.

1) A major key melody uses mostly the notes of the scale of that key. For our purposes in learning to craft a melody, you are advised to use *only* the notes of the major scale that you choose.

2) Choose a meter. 4/4, 3/4, or 6/8 are all typical and effective. Think of the 8-measure melody in two smaller phrases of four measures. Beginning the second phrase, in measure 5, the same way as measure 1, or slightly varied, will help demarcate the two phrases.

3) Create a correspondence between measures 2 and 6, 3 and 7, and 4 and 8. These may be as similar or varied as you like, but bear in mind that creating a recognizable correspondence between these pairs of measures will increase the melody's coherence.

4) The second four-measure phrase should be more elaborate than the first in order to create a sense of movement and climax in the melody. In Example 6-5, the highest note of the melody was obtained through an ascending scale that started on "a" in measure 5 and climbed to a "g," the high point of the melody, in measure 6. This creates a registral climax. You might also explore writing notes of shorter duration in the second phrase, which will create a sense of greater activity.

5) Begin your melody on the tonic note or a note associated with tonic. The associated notes are the third and fifth degrees of the scale, as we'll learn in Chapter 8. Note that the melody in Example 6-5 begins on the third note of the G Major scale, "b."

6) Avoid the tonic note to conclude measure 4. This will avoid a sense of finality better saved for the final measure. Good pitches to rest on in measure 4 are scale degrees 2, 5, or 7. Note that the final note of the first phrase, in measure 4 of our model example (6-5), is the second degree of the scale.

7) Conclude your melody on the tonic note or a note associated with it, the third or the fifth notes of the scale. Ending on the tonic will create the most convincing conclusion to your melody. Ending on the third degree is also conclusive, if a little less so. Ending on scale degree 5 is acceptable but is the least conclusive of the three choices. The other four scale degrees—2, 4, 6, and 7—are inconclusive and should be avoided.

8) Use primarily intervals of a second (major or minor in the key). This will create a smooth, singable, and memorable line. Use the other intervals more sparingly and for variety. Larger leaps tend to be dramatic, and you might want to save them for the climax of your melody.

9) Use a relatively small number of note values. Too many different note values, especially used arbitrarily, tend to diminish the coherence of a melody.

10) If you are feeling especially ambitious, see if you can incorporate a motive into your melody.

11) Use your ears to guide you! Your musical intuitions, honed through years of listening to music, are quite refined, even if you are just now learning how to represent these musical intuitions through notation. You **must** use the piano unless you can hear the notes in your head, which generally takes practice. Even if you don't play the piano, you can find the notes you've written because of your acquaintance with the keyboard. You may ignore some of the suggestions given above if your "ears" suggest a different way of proceeding.

EXERCISE 6-A

Name: _____

Major Key Melody

Write an 8-measure major key melody following the suggestions given in Chapter 6. You may choose any major key, as well as a time signature from among the following meters: 3/4, 4/4, or 6/8. The time signature needs only to be written on the first line. The key signature should appear on both lines. Do your work in pencil.

Writing Minor Key Melodies

In Chapter 6, we laid the foundations for writing effective major key melodies, and the guidelines explored there will serve the student well in writing minor key melodies. Your final project for this course will be to use both the major and minor key melodies that you've written in Chapters 6 and 7 to create a 24-measure piece with accompaniment. The two melodies we are exploring in these chapters have been composed to go together in a short piece, and the connection between the two will be explored in this chapter.

Your assignments for Chapters 6 and 7 are to compose an eight-measure major and minor key melody. As they will be combined in a final composition, they should be compatible with each other. One of the most effective ways to create compatibility is by composing the melodies in close-ly related keys. Keys are considered closely related when they share a similar number of accidentals. For our project, we are going to write a major key melody and minor key melody in either a rela-tive major/minor or parallel major/minor relationship to each other. As you remember from Chapter 4, relative major and minor keys share the same key signature, while parallel major and minor keys share the same tonic. If you chose C major for your melody in Exercise 6-A, you will write your minor key melody at the end of this chapter in A minor or C minor. If you chose F major for your melody in the previous chapter, then your choices for the minor key melody will be D minor or F minor. The choice of keys is yours. You will discover when you combine the melodies in the final composition project and accompany them with chords that these combinations of keys create a pleasing effect.

Our sample melody in Chapter 6 is in G major. Since the assignment stipulates that the minor key melody be either in the relative or parallel minor, we have a choice of either E minor or G minor. For the minor key model melody, we'll use E minor.

All of the suggestions for major key melody building in Chapter 6 are applicable to the creation of a minor key melody. There is one additional thing to bear in mind, however, as you construct your minor key melody. You will remember in Chapter 4 that whereas the major key scale is always the same, there are several scale forms for the minor key, and now we will have an opportunity to understand why. The natural minor scale was the scale of the minor key signature, without any alteration. The harmonic minor scale contained the notes that tend to supply the harmonies we use to accompany melodies, as will be further discussed in Chapters 10 and 12. The melodic minor had a different pattern ascending and descending, and it is this scale that we will be using to create our minor key melody.

Example 7-1 illustrates the melodic minor scale for the key in which we've chosen to write our minor key melody, E minor. As you remember from Chapter 4, the sixth and seventh degrees of the scale are raised by half-step in the ascending scale, and lowered (returned to the natural minor scale) by half-step in the descending scale. Now that we are dealing with concepts of melody, we can further explore why the scale is fashioned this way.

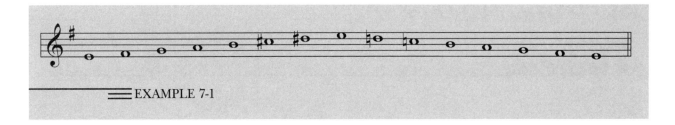

EXAMPLE 7-1

When the tonal system became increasingly codified at the beginning of the seventeenth century, the practice of writing in major or minor keys superceded the system that organized scales according to different modes. One of the important innovations of the tonal system was the development of a strong gravitational pull to the tonic note. As we observed in Chapter 4, the construction of scale degree 7 a **half-step** below the tonic note creates a stronger gravitational pull to scale degree 1 than does a whole-step. This strengthened gravitational pull to tonic is one of the features of the tonal system, and in tonal music of the seventeenth century to the present, you can generally count on this half-step relationship between the seventh and first degree of the scale.

In the natural minor scale, there is a whole step between scale degree 7 and 1. In order to create that half-step gravitational pull between those scale degrees, composers had to raise scale degree 7 by one-half-step to produce that half-step interval between 7 and 1. You'll notice in Example 7-1 that "d," which is natural in the key signature for E minor, gets raised one half-step to "d#." It is now a half-step from tonic, and will produce the desired pull to tonic when it is played. This explains why the seventh degree of the scale is raised. But we know that scale degree six is also raised in the melodic minor scale. The reason for this is that scales are generally constructed only of whole-steps and half-steps. This creates the smoothest line and the most singable one from the first note to last of the scale. But when we raise the scale degree 7 of the minor scale one half-step, we are left with a "gap" of three half-steps between scale degrees 6 and 7, and no longer have the smooth line produced when only whole-steps and half-steps separate the notes of a scale. If you play the two scales in Example 7-2, you will hear that the melodic minor scale (Example 7-2a) has a smoother contour than 7-2b, in which the sixth degree is not raised. This produces an augmented second between scale degrees 6 and 7, which is less smooth and more difficult to sing.

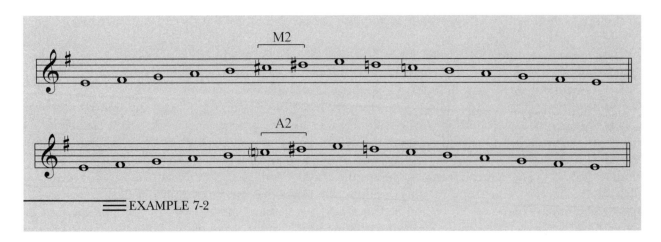

EXAMPLE 7-2

Typically, when composers write melodies that ascend through scale degrees 6 and 7 and return to 1, they use the melodic minor scale, that is, they raise scale degrees 6 and 7 one half-step to create the smooth line discussed above. However, when a pattern involves scale degree 7 *descending*, scale degree 7 is not raised, since it is moving away from the tonic rather than leaning up to it. This is why the descending melodic minor scale restores the pattern to the natural minor scale.

Look at the melody in Example 7-3. Notice in measure 2 that the melody involves scale degrees 5 ("b"), 6 ("c"), and 7 ("d"). The notes are ascending, but the pattern doesn't continue to the tonic ("e") but descends again. So even though the scale is ascending, scale degrees 6 and 7 are not raised since there is no return to tonic. If the melody had gone to "e," those notes would have been raised. In measure four, however, as the melody moves toward its conclusion, scale degrees 6, "c," and 7, "d," are raised a half-step as the scale returns to tonic, "e." If you play this example, you will see that raising scale degrees 6 and 7 in the last measure creates a strong gravitational pull back to tonic, stronger than if "c" and "d" remained natural, as they are in the key signature.

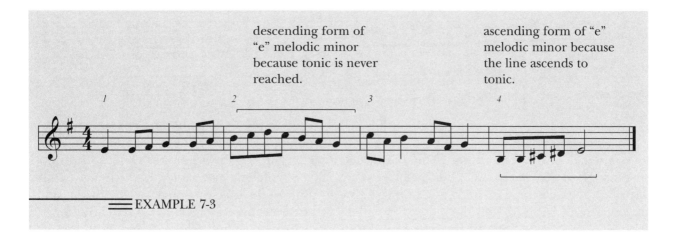

descending form of "e" melodic minor because tonic is never reached.

ascending form of "e" melodic minor because the line ascends to tonic.

EXAMPLE 7-3

When writing your melody, bear in mind that when scale degree 7 goes to 1, it should be raised, and that if the pattern returning to tonic involves scale degrees 6 and 7, both notes are raised a half-step, consistent with the ascending melodic minor scale. If the melody uses an ascending scale through degrees 6 and 7 but does not reach tonic, do not raise those scale degrees by half-step. When the music descends through 7 and 6, use the descending form of the melodic minor scale.

Observing the characteristics of the melody in Example 7-4 can serve as a guide to your own minor key melody. As in the major key melody in Chapter 6, this melody can be subdivided into two four-measure phrases. Measures 1 and 5, 2 and 6, 3 and 7, and 4 and 8 share rhythmic similarities.

Another thing you'll notice about measures 2 and 6, 3 and 7, and 4 and 8 are the melodic similarities. Measures 2 and 6 contain scale patterns, all whole- and half-steps, measure 2 descending and measure 3 ascending. Measures 3 and 7 use skips of primarily thirds and fourths, the skips in measure 3 mostly ascending, those in measure 7 mostly descending. Measures 4 and 8 use primarily the same notes, with one exception, and have exactly the same rhythm. All of these similarities make the second four-measure phrase sound like an elaboration of the first four-measure phrase, creating an orderly melody.

Like the major key melody in Chapter 6, the last note of measure 4 is scale degree 2, which gives the first phrase a sense of incompleteness that requires another phrase to create resolution and finality. The tonic note is eventually reached as the goal of measure 8. Also like the major key melody of the previous chapter, the starting note of both four-measure phrases is the tonic note ("e") in measure 5, and scale degree 5 in measure 1, one of the acceptable starting notes (along with scale degree 3) for beginning a phrase. As for which form of the scale to use, the ascending (raised 6 and 7) or descending (natural 6 and 7), notice in the example below that when the phrase is leaning to tonic "e," d is raised to "d#." When the goal of the phrase is not "e," "d" is not raised. In the fourth beat of measure 1 and first note of measure 2, we see that the goal is the tonic "e" in measure two. Even through the "f#" occurs between the "d#" and "e," "d" is raised to "d#" because the arrival point of the melody is tonic. Finally, note that the "skeletal" outlines of the melody in Example 7-4 in measures 5–8 (circled notes) form an ascending and descending minor scale from "e" to "a" back down to "e."

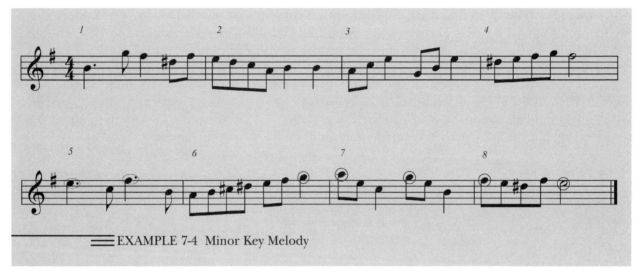

EXAMPLE 7-4 Minor Key Melody

Remember that your major and minor key melodies are going to be combined in your final composition, so whatever you can do to create a correspondence between them will add to the overall coherence of the composition. The only dotted quarter notes in the minor key melody occur in measures 1 and 5, and connect this melody to the major key melody in Chapter 6, which also begins each four-measure phrase with a dotted quarter note. You can see this by comparing the major key melody from Chapter 6 with the minor key melody, both reproduced in Example 7-5. In addition, the second phrase of both examples ascend through a scale pattern and reach the highest point of the melody, the major key melody in measure 6, the minor key melody in measure 7. These characteristics help unify the two melodies, as does the choice of relative major and minor keys.

EXAMPLE 7-5 Major and Minor Key Melodies

Suggestions for Writing a Minor Key Melody

The same suggestions for writing a major key melody will serve you well when writing your minor key melody. The only difference is that you will be concerned with the melodic minor scale ascending and descending, and making sure that when scale degree 7 goes to tonic, it is raised a half-step. Tips on how to handle the melodic minor are provided in (1) below.

1) A minor key melody uses the notes of the melodic minor scale. When ascending from scale degree 7 to 1, raise scale degree 7 one half-step. If the scale rises through scale degrees 6 and 7 to 1, 6 and 7 are both raised by a half-step, consistent with the ascending melodic minor scale. If scale degree 6 goes to 7 but begins to descend before reaching tonic, then 6 and 7 do not have to be raised. When the scale descends from tonic through scale degrees 7 and 6, these scale degrees are not raised, consistent with the descending melodic minor scales. While these are not hard and fast rules, they will help you to create sound tonal melodies. However, use your ears to determine what sounds best in creating your melody.

2) Use the same meter for the minor key melody that you did for the major key melody. Think of the 8-measure melody in two smaller phrases of four measures. Beginning the second phrase, in measure 5, the same way as measure 1, or slightly varied, will help demarcate the two phrases.

3) Create a correspondence between measures 2 and 6, 3 and 7, and 4 and 8. These may be as similar or varied as you like, but bear in mind that creating a recognizable correspondence between these pairs of measures will increase the melody's coherence.

4) The second four-measure phrase should be more elaborate than the first in order to create a sense of movement and climax in the melody. In Example 7-4, the highest note of the melody was obtained through an ascending scale that started on "a" in measure 6 and climbed to an "a," the high point of the melody, in measure 7. This creates a registral climax in approximately the same place as it occurred in the major key melody in Chapter 6.

5) Begin your melody on the tonic note or a note associated with tonic. The associated notes are the third and fifth degrees of the scale. Note that the melody in Example 7-4 begins on the fifth note of the E minor scale.

6) Avoid the tonic note to conclude measure 4. This will preclude a sense of finality better saved for the final measure. Good pitches to rest on in measure 4 are scale degrees 2, 5, or 7. Note that the final note of the first phrase, in measure 4 of our model example (7-4), is the second degree of the scale, as it was in measure 4 of the major key melody.

7) Conclude your melody on the tonic note or a note associated with it, the third or the fifth notes of the scale. Ending on the tonic will create the most convincing conclusion to your melody. Ending on the third degree is also conclusive, if a little less so. Ending on scale degree 5 is acceptable but is the least conclusive of the three choices. The other four scale degrees—2, 4, 6, and 7—are inconclusive and should be avoided.

8) Use primarily intervals of a second (major or minor in the key). This will create a smooth, singable, and memorable line. Use the other intervals more sparingly and for variety. Larger leaps tend to be dramatic, and you might want to save them for the climax of your melody. In the minor key melody in Example 7-4, over half of the intervals are seconds, although there are greater and more dramatic leaps in the rest of the melody than there are in the major key melody.

9) Use a relatively small number of note values. Too many different note values, especially used arbitrarily, tend to diminish the coherence of a melody.

10) If you are feeling especially ambitious, see if you can incorporate a motive into your melody.

11) For both your major and minor key melodies, use your ears to guide you! Again, use the piano to choose pitches. You may ignore some of the suggestions given above if your "ears" suggest a different way of proceeding.

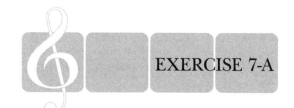

EXERCISE 7-A

Name: _____

Minor Key Melody

Write an 8-measure minor key melody following the suggestions given in Chapter 7. Choose the relative or parallel minor key of the major key in which your melody in Chapter 6 was composed. The time signature should also be the same as that chosen for your major key melody. As with your major key melody, the time signature needs only to be written on the first line. The key signature should appear on both lines. Do your work in pencil.

Triads and Chords

To this point we have dealt mostly with notes played singly. One of the central attributes of Western music is the development of **harmony**, which is the term that describes the vertical dimension of music, that is, groups of notes played together and considered as harmonic units.

Texture in music describes the interaction of the horizontal and vertical dimensions of the art, that is, the interaction of melody and melody and melody and harmony. There are three primary textures, **monophonic, homophonic**, and **polyphonic.** These terms are adjectives, and are used with the word "texture," as in a "polyphonic texture." They also have noun forms, monophony, homophony, and polyphony. A monophonic texture involves one line of music without pitched accompaniment. Gregorian chants are monophonic, for example, and when "Happy Birthday" is sung without accompaniment, no matter by how many people, that is a monophonic texture as well. Music with homophonic textures evolved around the turn of the seventeenth century. This kind of music features a single prominent line or melody, accompanied by groups of notes played together as an important, but background, texture. Most opera is homophonic in texture, that is, one person sings while the orchestra plays combinations of notes as accompaniment. Most pop and rock songs are homophonic, piano or guitars playing chords against a solo voice. Jazz ballads are homophonic. Most of the tonal music composed since 1600 has been primarily homophonic in texture. Preceding the advent of music with homophonic textures was polyphonic music, which reached its zenith in the work of Johann Sebastian Bach, who died in 1750. In a polyphonic texture, two or more melody lines are juxtaposed (the term "poly" means "many"), with the resultant sound producing harmony. Most music with a polyphonic texture has three or four melody lines (called "voices" in polyphonic music whether sung or played), although there has been music written with only two lines (occasionally) and six lines (more often).

When notes are grouped together to produce harmonies, we call those groupings **chords.** The music that results from polyphonic and homophonic textures is made up of chords, whether the result of a group of notes being played together by one instrument (a pianist, for example, playing three notes simultaneously), or the combination of independent lines producing several pitches at once. For our purposes in learning about chords, the kind of texture we'll be dealing with is a homophonic texture, that is, the groupings of notes that are played simultaneously as an accompaniment to a melody line. Chords in tonal music usually have three notes, called **triads.** Sometimes a fourth note is added, and these four-note chords are called **seventh chords**, for reasons to be discussed later. Triads and seventh chords can be called, generically, chords.

Whether a triad or seventh chord, the construction of chords follows the same principles. Notes are arranged in thirds, which is to say that if the bottom note is on a line, the two or three notes above it will also be on a line. If the bottom note is on a space, the top two or three notes are on a space. When notes are arranged in this order of thirds, then the note on which the chord is based and for which it is named is on the bottom. That note is called the **root**, as everything rises from it.

In Example 8-1, three chords are displayed. The first two are triads, the third is a seventh chord. The notes above the root are named for their relationship to the root. The note at an interval of a third above the root is called the **third** of the chord. The note above that is called the **fifth**, because it sits as an interval of a fifth above the root. An added fourth note, above the fifth (Example 8-1c below), is called the **seventh** because it sits at an interval of a seventh above the root. Note that all adjacent notes are an interval of a third apart, and that that being the case, the notes are all on lines or on spaces. When a chord is stacked in thirds, we say the chord is in **root** position, because the root is in the lowest "voice." The lowest note of a stack of notes is called the **bass.**

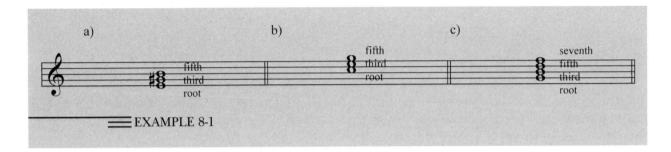

EXAMPLE 8-1

Triad Qualities

There are four qualities of triads, that is, three-note chords with a different arrangement of thirds and distinctive, and different, sonorities. All of these triad qualities exist "naturally" when notes of a scale are combined in thirds. We are already familiar with terms used to describe triads from our work with intervals. The four triad qualities are called **major, minor, diminished,** and **augmented.** The abbreviations are M (major), m (minor), d (diminished), and A (augmented).

The Major Triad

The **major** triad consists of a major third (four half-steps) between the root and third and a minor third (three half-steps) between the third and fifth. The interval between the root and fifth is a perfect fifth. This is a common triad in tonal music.

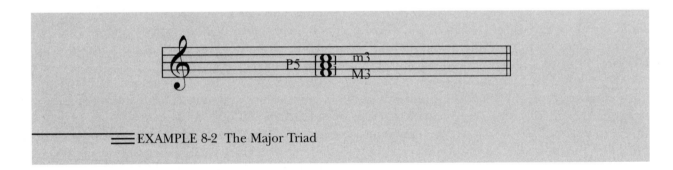

EXAMPLE 8-2 The Major Triad

The Minor Triad

The **minor** triad reverses the order of thirds, with the minor third between the root and third and a major third between the third and fifth. Like the major triad, there is a perfect fifth between the root and fifth. Because between the root and fifth there is a perfect fifth, major and minor triads are stable. They can be sonorities of resolution, concluding a passage or a piece. The minor triad is also a frequently heard chord in tonal music.

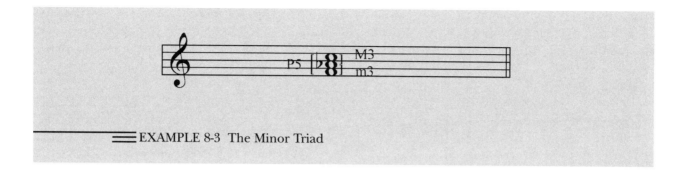

EXAMPLE 8-3 The Minor Triad

The Diminished Triad

The **diminished** triad contains two minor thirds. It is called diminished because the resultant interval between the root and fifth is a *diminished* fifth (six rather than seven half-steps). The diminished chord occurs less frequently in tonal music, partly because it is an unstable chord, which means it needs to resolve to another chord.

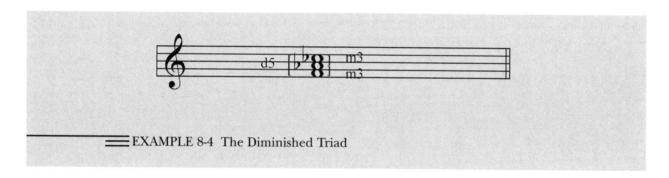

EXAMPLE 8-4 The Diminished Triad

The Augmented Triad

The augmented triad contains two major thirds. It is referred to as augmented because the resultant interval between the root and fifth is an *augmented* fifth. This chord occurs very infrequently, for reasons that will become apparent in Chapters 9 and 10. Like the diminished triad, the augmented triad is unstable because the interval between the root and fifth is not perfect.

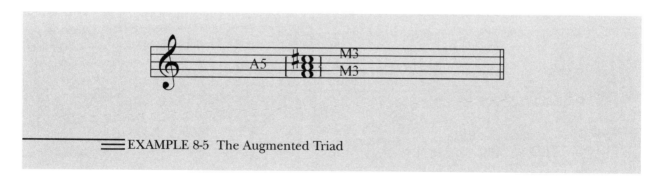

EXAMPLE 8-5 The Augmented Triad

As we shall see in Chapter 9, these chords result when the notes of the major and minor scale are stacked in thirds.

In preparation for the homework at the end of the chapter, let's build a major triad on "gb." The first step is to write two thirds above the root. Visually, this is straightforward: if the root is on a space, then the next two notes are also placed on the adjacent spaces above the root. If the root is on a line, as is the case with "gb," then the third and fifth are placed on the two adjacent lines above the root. Example 8-6 illustrates (a), the given root, and (b), the placement of thirds above the root.

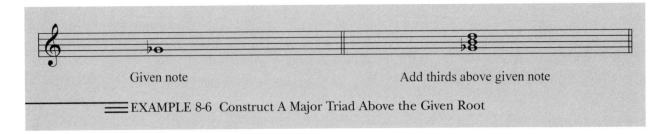

Given note   Add thirds above given note

EXAMPLE 8-6 Construct A Major Triad Above the Given Root

Now apply the pattern for the major triad: a major third above the root and a minor third between the root and fifth. The major third requires four half-steps in the interval. Between "gb" and "b" is five half-steps, so the "b" must be flatted to make four half-steps, the interval in a major third. Now "bb" is the third of the triad, and the "d" must be adjusted to make a minor third above "bb." "Bb" to "d" is four half-steps and a minor third is three, so "d" must also be flatted to create three half-steps. The correct notes for the Gb major triad are "gb," "bb," and "db," as illustrated in Example 8-7. If you write the two thirds above the root correctly, the quality of the fifth will also be correct.

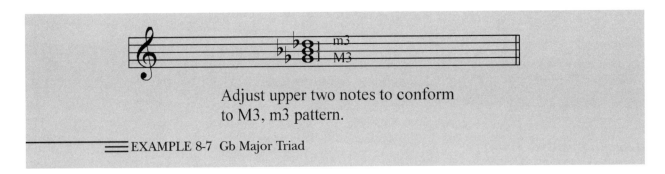

Adjust upper two notes to conform
to M3, m3 pattern.

EXAMPLE 8-7 Gb Major Triad

Let's do one more example step by step. Write an augmented triad above the given root. First, write the third and fifth above the root (see Example 8-8b). Since the root is on a space, the two adjacent chord tones will also be on spaces.

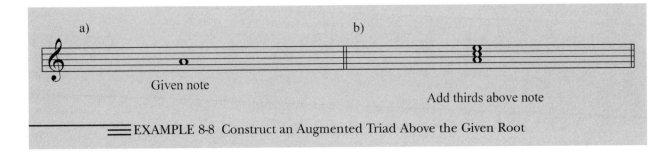

a)   b)

Given note

Add thirds above note

EXAMPLE 8-8 Construct an Augmented Triad Above the Given Root

Now apply the pattern for an augmented triad: two major thirds, one between the root and third, the other between the third and fifth. As you begin your practice, it will be helpful to write the intervals that you are constructing, as you see below. From "a" to "c" is only three half-steps, or a minor third. To make it a major third, you have to expand the interval by a half-step, so "c" is raised to "c#." Now "c#" is your starting point. From "c#" to "e" is only a minor third (three half-steps). Since the augmented triad calls for a major third between the third and fifth, that interval must be expanded by a half-step to change the minor third into a major third. You raise the "e" a half-step to "e#." Now you have constructed an augmented triad. If you construct the two major thirds in an augmented triad, the result will be an augmented fifth between the root and the fifth. Remember to always begin by writing the triad tones above the root. That way you will avoid incorrect enharmonic spellings.

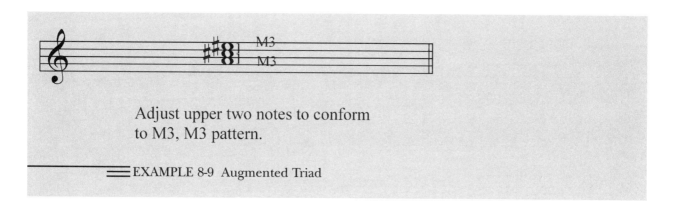

Adjust upper two notes to conform
to M3, M3 pattern.

EXAMPLE 8-9 Augmented Triad

This would be a good time to memorize the pattern for the four chord qualities. They are comprised of the following intervals above the root:

Major triad: M3, m3   resultant fifth: perfect
Minor triad: m3, M3   resultant fifth: perfect
Diminished triad: m3, m3   resultant fifth: diminished
Augmented triad: M3, M3   resultant fifth: augmented

Let's take a moment to practice constructing one of each triad quality before doing the homework at the end of the chapter.

Construct a major triad above the given root.

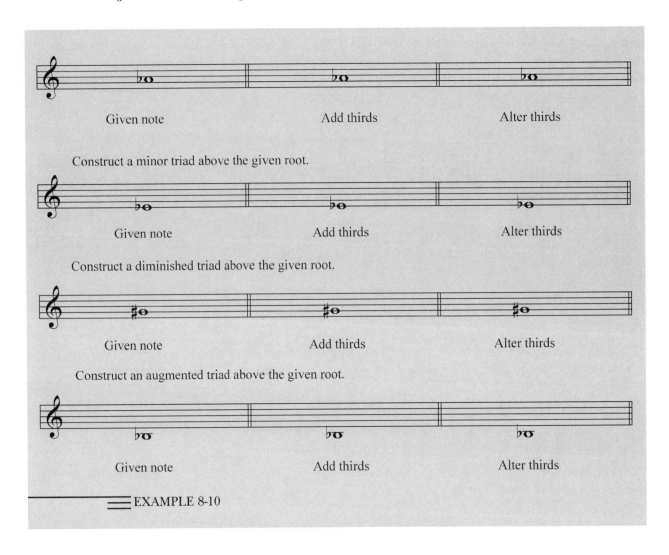

Construct a minor triad above the given root.

Construct a diminished triad above the given root.

Construct an augmented triad above the given root.

EXAMPLE 8-10

Seventh Chords

Although the main chordal building block of tonal music is the triad, composers often add an additional note to the triad to create a seventh chord. The triad has a root, third, and fifth. When we add a third above the fifth, we create the interval of a seventh above the root. This seventh will either be major, minor, or diminished, depending on the function of the chord to which it is added. (This will be discussed further in Chapter 9.)

To major triads, a major or minor seventh may be added above the root. To minor triads, a major or minor seventh may be added above the root, although the major seventh is very rare. To diminished triads, a minor or diminished seventh may be added above the root. Augmented triads will occasionally have a minor seventh added above the root. It is important to point out that these sevenths (except for the major seventh added to the minor triad) occur naturally when notes are stacked in thirds above the roots in major and minor keys. Example 8-11 demonstrates the typical sevenths that are added to triads. Notice that most of the chords are named with the triad quality first and the quality of the seventh second (a major chord with a major seventh above the root is labeled a major major seventh (MM7). In the case of the diminished chords, there is a different terminology. Adding a minor seventh above a diminished triad makes it a **half diminished seventh chord**, the symbol of which is a circle with a diagonal line through it:º. Adding a diminished seventh above a diminished triad makes it a **fully diminished seventh chord**, the symbol of which is a circle without the diagonal line through it: °. Note in Example 8-11 that there are two major chords with sevenths added, two minor chords with sevenths added, two diminished triads with sevenths added, and one augmented chord, that adds a minor seventh above the root.

Looking at the chords individually, you'll note that (a) the MM seventh chord is a major triad and major seventh above the root. (b) the Mm chord is a major triad with a minor seventh above the root. (c) the mM seventh chord is a minor triad with a major seventh above the root (rare in Classical music). (d) the mm seventh chord is a minor triad with a minor seventh above the root. (e) the half diminished seventh chord is a diminished triad with a minor seventh above the root. (f) the fully diminished seventh chord is a diminished triad with a diminished seventh above the root. (Note that in order to create a diminished seventh above "c," or nine half-steps, "b" must be made double flat.) (g) the Aug/m seventh chord is an augmented triad with a minor seventh above the root. (This chord appears in Classical music of the nineteenth Century).

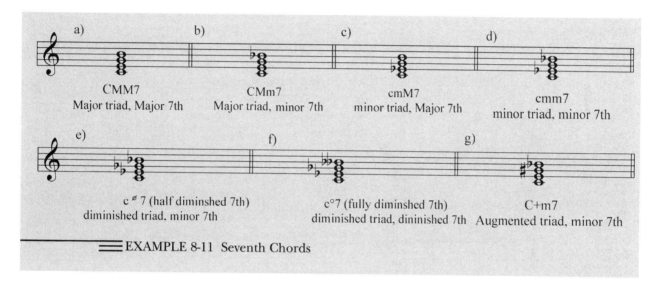

EXAMPLE 8-11 Seventh Chords

Let's practice constructing one of these seventh chords in preparation for the homework at the end of the chapter. In order to do this and the subsequent homework, you'll need to review and then memorize the formula for the construction of the following seventh chords:

MM7: Major triad, Major 7th above the root
Mm7: Major triad, minor 7th above the root
mM7: minor triad, Major 7th above the root
mm7: minor triad, minor 7th above the root
ø7: diminished triad, minor 7th above the root
°7: diminished triad, diminished 7th above the root

Say you are asked to construct a mm7 (minor minor seventh) chord on the root "eb" (see Example 8-12). Follow the same procedures you followed in the construction of the triads. You will begin by writing the notes of the chord above the root, but add a fourth note to the stack (Example 8-12b). Remember that if the root is on a line, all the other chord tones must be on adjacent lines; if the root is on a space, all the other chord tones must be on adjacent spaces. Then use your formula to create a minor triad: minor third and major third (Example 8-12c). In Example 8-12d, the seventh called for is the minor seventh above the root. "Eb" to "d" is a major seventh (eleven half-steps), so "d" must be lowered by half-step to "db," ten half-steps, the interval of the minor seventh.

Construct a mm7 (minor minor 7th chord above the root).

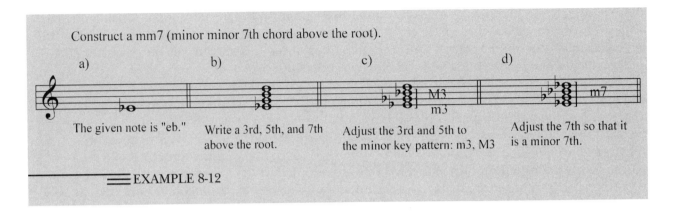

a)	b)	c)	d)

The given note is "eb."

Write a 3rd, 5th, and 7th above the root.

Adjust the 3rd and 5th to the minor key pattern: m3, M3

Adjust the 7th so that it is a minor 7th.

═══ EXAMPLE 8-12

Use Example 8-13 to practice writing seventh chords. Follow the procedures outlined above.

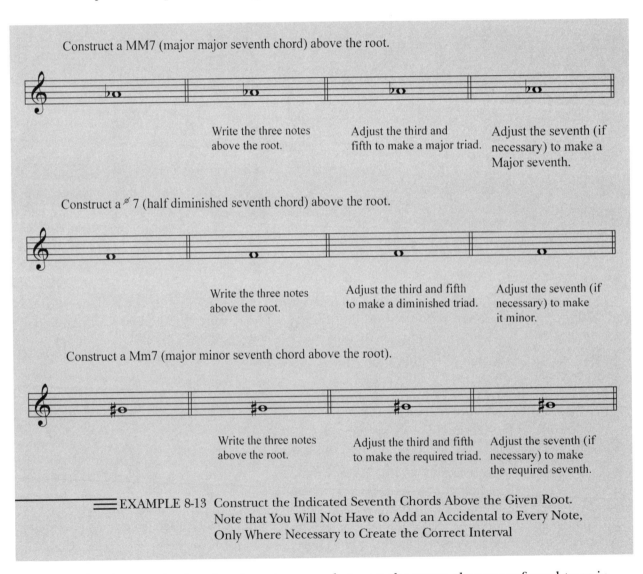

Construct a MM7 (major major seventh chord) above the root.

Write the three notes above the root.

Adjust the third and fifth to make a major triad.

Adjust the seventh (if necessary) to make a Major seventh.

Construct a ⌀7 (half diminished seventh chord) above the root.

Write the three notes above the root.

Adjust the third and fifth to make a diminished triad.

Adjust the seventh (if necessary) to make it minor.

Construct a Mm7 (major minor seventh chord above the root).

Write the three notes above the root.

Adjust the third and fifth to make the required triad.

Adjust the seventh (if necessary) to make the required seventh.

═══ EXAMPLE 8-13 Construct the Indicated Seventh Chords Above the Given Root.
Note that You Will Not Have to Add an Accidental to Every Note,
Only Where Necessary to Create the Correct Interval

When chords are voiced so that there is no gap between the notes, they are referred to as in **close position,** that is, the notes of the chords are as close together as possible. When the notes are "spread out," that is, they are not written as close together as possible, the chord is referred to as in **open position.** Example 8-14a illustrates a close position E Major triad, while 8-14b illustrates an open position triad. In the first, the notes "e," "g#," and "b" are as close together as possible. In the second, a more realistic voicing in music and one that produces more sonorous results than the close position spacing, the chord tones are spread out. There is a space between "e" in the **bass** (the lowest voice) and "b" in the **tenor** (the next lowest voice). The lower pitch on the treble clef, the **alto,** is a "g#," filling in the third of the chord. Now we have all three pitches of the triad, but because textures in tonal music typically have four parts, one of the notes of a triad will be repeated, or **doubled** in such textures. The best pitch to double in a root position triad (that is, where the root is the lowest "voice") is the root, and we find that in the highest voice, the **soprano.** Note that in a four part texture, especially when written for voices, there are two notes in the bass clef and two notes in the treble clef. In order from lowest to highest, these voices (whether sung or played, musical lines are referred to as "voices") are labeled bass, tenor, alto, and soprano. Typically, the two voices in the bass clef are sung by male voices, while the top two lines are sung by female voices.

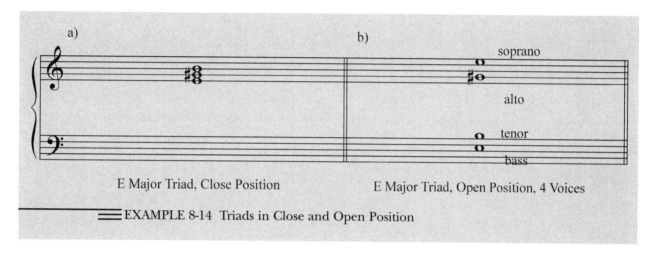

E Major Triad, Close Position   E Major Triad, Open Position, 4 Voices

EXAMPLE 8-14 Triads in Close and Open Position

When identifying triads and chords in open position, it is necessary to "reduce" these chords to close position. In Example 8-15, we see a triad and a seventh chord, both in open position in the standard 4-note voicing. In order to see what these chords are and to identify their quality, it is helpful to rearrange the notes in close position, beginning with the bass note and writing the successive notes above that bass. In Example 8-15a, the open position notes are rearranged on top of the bass in close position. All notes must be accounted for, but repeated notes (the "ab") need only be represented once. Looking at the intervallic pattern, we can see that the interval between the root and third is a M3, and the interval between the third and fifth is a m3. That is the pattern for a major triad, so we label the chord AbM. Reducing the notes to close position makes it easy to see the intervallic pattern until the musician becomes more practiced at identifying chords in open position. In Example 8-15b, we see a seventh chord in open position and its rearrangement in close position beginning with the bass note. Once it is rearranged, we see that it is a root position seventh chord (that is, the root of the chord is in the bass) and can label it accordingly. Its intervallic pattern contains a m3 between the root and third, a M3 between the third and fifth, and a m7 between the root and seventh. This is the pattern for a mm7 chord. The root of the chord is "f," so we label it fmm7. Remember when labeling chords that when the triad is major and augmented, we use upper case letters to describe the root. When the triad is minor or diminished, we use lower case letters to describe the root. Note that when we describe a triad (Example 8-15a) that we only need one letter to describe it because a triad is either Major, minor, diminished, or Augmented. In a MM7, Mm7, mM7, and mm7 chord, we use the first letter to describe the quality of the triad and the second to describe the interval between the root and the seventh. For diminished seventh chords, the terminology is different. We use a circle (rather than a letter) and a 7 to describe a fully diminished seventh chord, and a circle with a diagonal line running through it and a 7 to describe a half-diminished seventh chord. The Augmented triad with the minor seventh is symbolized as +m7.

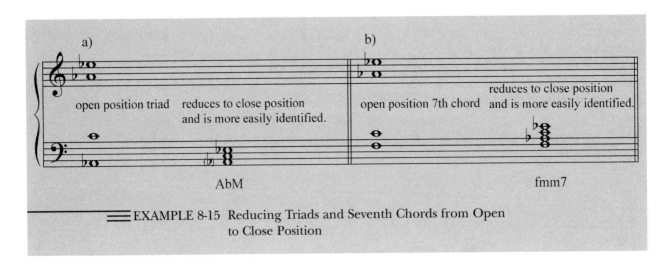

open position triad   reduces to close position and is more easily identified.

open position 7th chord   reduces to close position and is more easily identified.

AbM

fmm7

EXAMPLE 8-15   Reducing Triads and Seventh Chords from Open to Close Position

Practice reducing open position triads and seventh chords and label them in the four examples below.

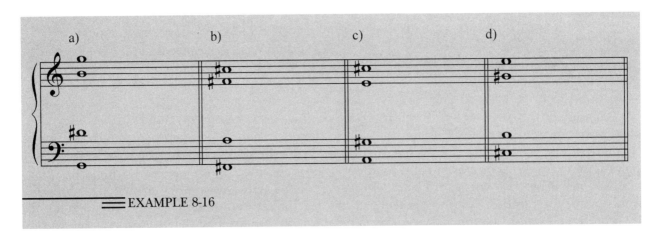

EXAMPLE 8-16

Chapters 9 and 10 will explore the harmonic contexts in which triads and seventh chords appear.

EXERCISE 8-B

Name: _____

Construct the indicated triads on the given roots. When you are finished,
play them on the piano to acquaint yourself with the different sonorities.

M = Major, m = minor, o = diminished, + = Augmented

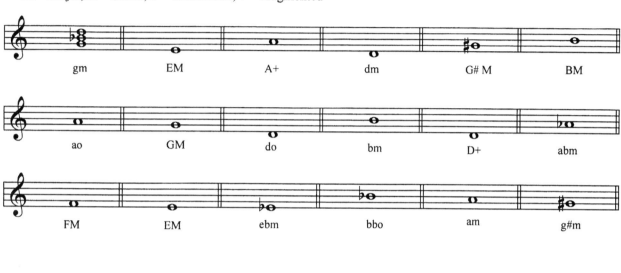

gm   EM   A+   dm   G#M   BM

ao   GM   do   bm   D+   abm

FM   EM   ebm   bbo   am   g#m

gm   co   bbm   abo   EM   FM

fo   B+   gm   bbo   C+   cm

f#o   F#M   fm   AbM   c#o   C#M

GM   ebm   C#M   F#+   c#m   G#+

d#o   F+   dm   Eb+   DbM   AM

TRIADS AND CHORDS 𝄢: 129

EXERCISE 8-C

Name: _____

Identify the root and quality (M, m,d, A) of the following triads. Use upper case for Major, lower case for minor, lower case with a o for diminished, and uppercase with a + for Augmented. Play them on the piano to acquaint yourself with the different sonorities.

g# ○

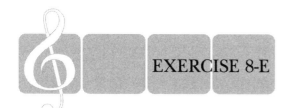

EXERCISE 8-E

Name: _____

Reduce the following open position triads to close position and identify them by root and quality. For seventh chords, write MM7, Mm7, mM7, mm7, °7 or ⌀7.

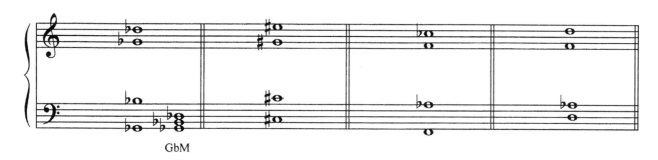

GbM

Reduce the following open position seventh chords to close position and identify them by root and seventh quality.

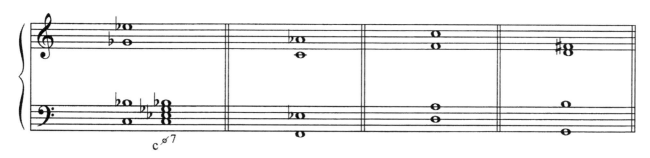

c⌀7

Root Position Chords in Major Keys

All of the triads and all but one of the seventh chords studied in the previous chapter occur naturally when notes of the major and minor scales are stacked in thirds. In this chapter, the chords of the major scale will be considered in context.

The easiest way to examine triad qualities in a major key is to write a scale and add thirds and fifths above the root of each member of the chosen scale. In Example 9-1, a D Major scale is shown. Each scale degree serves as the root of a triad, and the thirds and fifths are notes in the key. You'll notice that each chord consists of two thirds and that these form either Major, minor, or diminished chords. The thirds are indicated in the example, and you can see that the chord built on the first degree of the scale stacks, from bottom to top, a M3 and then a m3, the formula for the Major triad. The chord built on the second degree of the scale is stacked from bottom to top as a m3 and M3. This is the formula for a minor triad. The triad built on the third degree of the scale also stacks from top to bottom as a m3 and M3, another minor triad, and so on. These chords are labeled with their root and triad quality in Example 9-1. Remember that major triads are labeled with an upper case letter, minor triads with a lower case letter, and diminished triads with a lower case letter with a circle to the right.

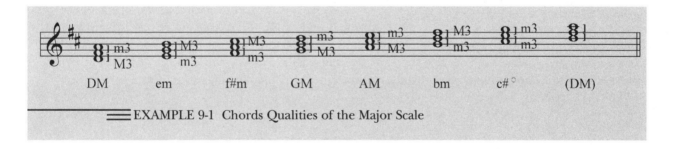

DM   em   f#m   GM   AM   bm   c#°   (DM)

EXAMPLE 9-1 Chords Qualities of the Major Scale

Throughout the book, we have discussed the strong gravitational pull that is at the heart of the tonal system. When we played a major scale and stopped on scale degree seven, we experienced a strong sense of irresolution. Resolving to the tonic a half-step above the seventh degree of the scale to the tonic created a sense of arrival. This sense of tension and resolution also exists among the chords in major and minor keys. The chord of resolution in tonal music is the tonic chord, the first degree of the scale with the third and fifth notes of the scale stacked on top of it. When composers want to create a sense of finality, they write a tonic triad; no other triad will give the same sense of complete closure. The entire tonal system is built around the tonic as the central, "home" base. As such, the chord built on the first degree of a major scale is labeled I. As it is a major chord, it is represented with an upper case roman numeral. All the notes of the scale are labeled in a way that relates back to I. The chord built on the second degree of the scale is labeled ii, the chord built on the third degree of the scale iii, and so on. (You will also notice that what determines whether the roman numeral is upper case, lower case, or lower case with a circle after it depends on whether the chord is major, minor, or diminished.) The chord naturally occurring on I, IV, and V in a major key without alterations will always be major; ii, iii, and vi will always be minor; the chord built on vii° will always be diminished.

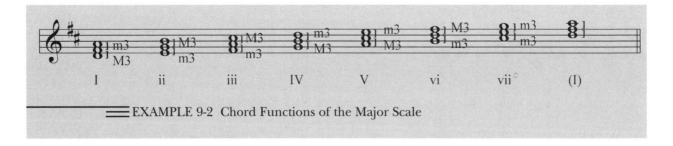

EXAMPLE 9-2 Chord Functions of the Major Scale

Every major scale will have the same pattern of triad qualities if all the stacked notes are derived from the major scale. This consistency makes it easy to know chord qualities for every note of the major scale. You should memorize the qualities for each of the triads of the major scale. This will be useful when we begin our chapter on harmonic analysis. The chord qualities are as follows:

Major chords of the major scale: I, IV, V
Minor chords of the major scale: ii, iii, vi
Diminished chord of the major scale: vii°

Composers string together series of chords, which constitute the harmonic backbone of their music. These chord series are called **progressions.** We will learn more about typical progressions in tonal music in Chapter 11. In this chapter, we will learn how to do a harmonic analysis of root position triads and seventh chords.

We begin by identifying triads in a tonal context. A favored texture in music is four notes or "voices." This gives the composer the latitude to expand the triads to seventh chords, which require four voices, and allows him or her to double one note in each triad, which creates a full sonority. Example 9-3 demonstrates a typical progression in tonal music. Note that there are four notes, in the bass, tenor, alto, and soprano. Because there are only three different notes in a triad as all of these chords are triads, one of those three notes is doubled in the texture. Note that the key of D Major is indicated underneath the bottom staff with a large D followed by a colon.

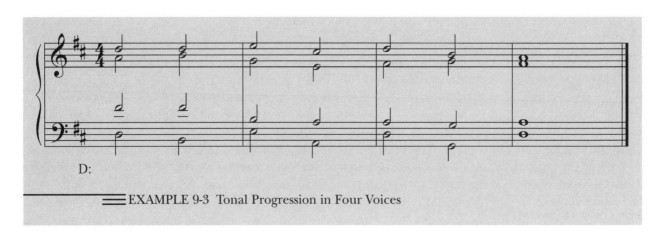

EXAMPLE 9-3 Tonal Progression in Four Voices

To understand the progression of chords in relationship to the tonic triad, we do a **harmonic analysis**, which is an examination of the sequence of chords by identifying the roman numeral and quality of each chord. To do this, we continue the lessons learned in Chapter 8. Until the eye becomes practiced at identifying chords in open position, reducing the open position triads to close position is the easiest way to examine the progression. It is also useful to reproduce all of the triads of the major scale in sequence. The triads of the D Major scale in Example 9-2 is reproduced in Example 9-4 for easy reference.

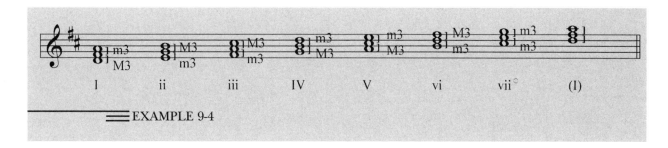

EXAMPLE 9-4

Example 9-5 reduces the open, four-part texture into triads in close position. You'll notice that doubled notes (for example, the "d" in the first chord) are not written twice and that the chord is stacked on the bass note. For example, in the first triad, the "f#" in the tenor voice is brought down an octave to a third above the bass. The "a" in the alto voice is then brought down to the "a" above that. As we already have the "d" of the triad represented in the bass, we ignore the "d" in the soprano. This gives us a close position triad in which the root is "d." We now look at our triads in Example 9-4 and look for the triad whose root is "d." That is the tonic triad, and we label it with an upper case roman numeral I. Continuing to the second chord in the progression, we again stack all of the chord tones of that triad above the bass note. The "f#" of the tenor is brought down to its closest possible position above the "b" in the bass, the "b" of the alto is ignored (we already have a "b" in the bass), and the "d" of the soprano part is brought down to its closest position above the bass. As there is a note on "b," "d," and "f#," this triad too is in close position. Now we look for the triad whose root is "b" and see that it is a vi chord. We know too that a vi chord in a major key is minor, so we represent it with a lower case roman numeral. We continue this procedure for each of the triads in the progression and come up with the following order of triads: I-vi-ii-V-I-IV-I. Play this progression on the piano. You'll see it has a logic as it moves steadily back to the tonic triad at the beginning of measure 3, and reinforces tonic in measure 4. Note the missing fifth in the sixth chord.

EXAMPLE 9-5 Roman Numeral Analysis

Prior to tackling the homework at the end of this chapter, let's practice reducing the triads in Example 9-7 to close position and identifying them by roman numeral. The example is in Bb Major. The first thing you'll need to do is write the notes of the Bb Major scale and construct triads with each scale tone as the root in Example 9-6. Then, write in the pattern of roman numerals from I-I, being careful to reflect the quality of each triad with the symbols indicated in Example 9-4. Proceeding to Example 9-7, reduce each triad to close position above the root. Once you have done that, check the root against your scale of triads in Example 9-6 and write in the sequence of roman numerals.

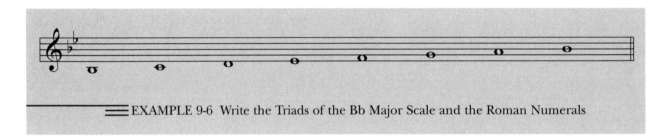

EXAMPLE 9-6 Write the Triads of the Bb Major Scale and the Roman Numerals

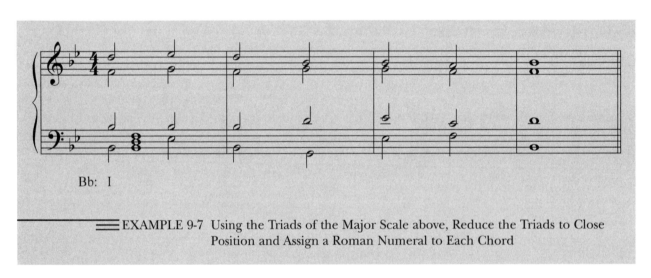

Bb: I

EXAMPLE 9-7 Using the Triads of the Major Scale above, Reduce the Triads to Close Position and Assign a Roman Numeral to Each Chord

Although triads dominate the textural landscape of tonal music, seventh chords appear with frequency, especially the seventh chord built on scale degree V. Example 9-8 illustrates the triad and seventh quality of seventh chords built on each degree of the scale. Underneath each chord is the roman numeral designation for the seventh, beneath which is the make-up of the chord. In all but the chord built on scale degree seven, the first letter refers to the quality of the triad, the second to the interval of the seventh above the root. In the case of the chord built on the seventh degree of the scale, the circle with the diagonal line through it is the symbol for half-diminished. The seventh chord built on scale degree I is a major chord with a major seventh above the root. The triads and sevenths above the root are given in the table below and are illustrated in Example 9-8.

I7 = Major triad, Major seventh
ii7 = minor triad, minor seventh
iii7 = minor triad, minor seventh
IV7 = Major triad, major seventh
V7 = Major triad, minor seventh
vi7 = minor triad, minor seventh
vii$^{\varnothing}$7 = diminished triad, minor seventh

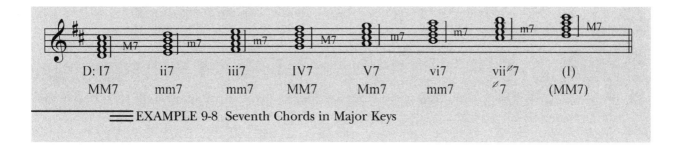

EXAMPLE 9-8 Seventh Chords in Major Keys

Sevenths may be added to any triad of the scale. The most frequently occurring seventh chord by far in tonal music is the V7 (called the dominant seventh). The other triads in a major key that occur with some frequency adding a seventh are the ii7 and vii°7, the former more frequent. Neither of these chords is heard as frequently as the V7, which is very common in tonal music. Sevenths built on iii, iv, or vi are less common, a seventh added to a I chord occurs infrequently in classical music. When building your triad qualities, it might be useful to add sevenths only to those chords that are most frequently heard as seventh chords: ii7, V7, and vii°7.

Your chart of triads and seventh chords in succession beginning with the I chord now looks as indicated below. Again, although all of the triads can have a seventh added, ii7, V7 and vii°7 are the ones that occur most frequently, and thus are represented in the Example 9-9.

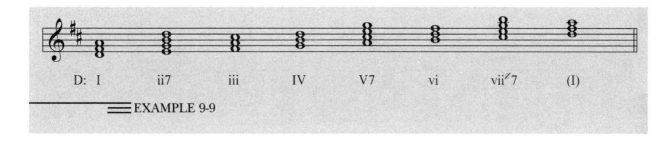

EXAMPLE 9-9

Now that we have added seventh chords, we can analyze music that contains sevenths. When chords are in root position, we indicate that there is a seventh in the chord by adding the numeral "7" after the chord. Let's examine the chorale from Example 9-5. It has been altered to add sevenths to two chords. Note that in the case of the V7, there are two "a's," a "c#" and a "g." The fifth of the chord is missing. Sometimes composers leave out the fifth of a chord when doing so makes each voice move smoothly from chord to chord. Know that when there is a root, third, and seventh and the fifth is missing, the root of the chord is still the note after which the chord is named.

EXAMPLE 9-10 Chorale with Seventh Chords

Before doing the homework at the end of the chapter, let's practice reducing the triads and seventh chords in Example 9-12 and identifying them by roman numeral. The example is in E Major. The first thing you'll need to do is write the notes of the E Major scale and construct triads with each scale tone as the root in Example 9-11. Build a seventh on the triads of ii, V, and vii°. Then, write in the pattern of roman numerals from I-I, being careful to reflect the quality of each triad with the symbols indicated in Example 9-11. Then reduce the chords in Example 9-12 and write in the roman numerals. In the case of seventh chords, add a "7" after the roman numeral.

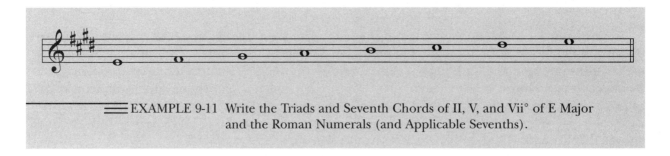

EXAMPLE 9-11 Write the Triads and Seventh Chords of II, V, and Vii° of E Major and the Roman Numerals (and Applicable Sevenths).

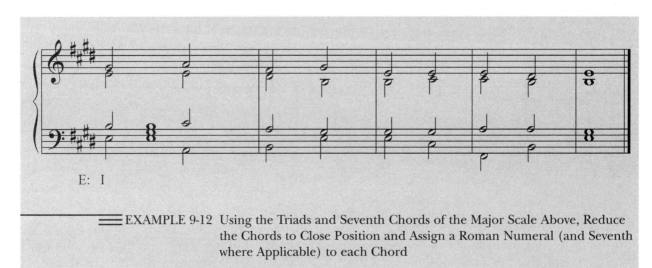

EXAMPLE 9-12 Using the Triads and Seventh Chords of the Major Scale Above, Reduce the Chords to Close Position and Assign a Roman Numeral (and Seventh where Applicable) to each Chord

EXERCISE 9-A

Name: _MjCW_

Answer the questions below.

1) Major triads are represented by roman numerals in (upper) or lower case. (Circle one.)

2) Minor triads are represented by roman numerals in upper or (lower) case. (Circle one.)

3) Diminished triads are represented by roman numerals in upper or (lower) case (circle one) followed by the symbol ____ .

4) Augmented triads are represented by roman numerals in (upper) or lower case (circle one) followed by the symbol ____ .

5) In a major key, _1_ , _4_ , and _5_ are major triads.

6) In a major key, _2_ , _3_ and _6_ are minor triads.

7) In a major key, _7_ is a diminished triad.

8) In a major key, there is a M7 between the root and seventh of the ____ and ____ chords.

9) In a major key, there is a m7 between the root and seventh of the ____ , ____ , ____ , ____ and ____ chords.

10) In a major key, the three most common chords to add a seventh to the triad in tonal classical music are ____ , ____ , and ____ .

11) Write the roman numeral symbols for the seven chords of the major key. Add 7 for the chords built on the second, fifth, and seventh degrees of the scale.

_I_   _ii7_   _iii_   _IV_   _V7_   _vi_   _vii7_

Read chat.
at 10

EXERCISE 9-C

Name: _____

For each exercise, on a separate sheet of staff paper, write all the triads for I, iii, IV, and vi, and seventh chords for ii, V, and vii in the indicated keys and label each chord with a roman numeral and 7 where applicable. Then reduce the open position chords in each exercise to close position and indicate the roman numerals. Add a 7 where necessary. Unlike the previous exercises, these chords are in progressions. Remember that there might sometimes not be a fifth in a chord. Label the chord with the roman numeral of the lowest note of a stacked third.

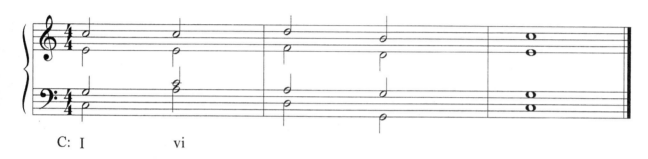

C: I   vi

G:

Bb:

EXERCISE 9-C
(CONTINUED)

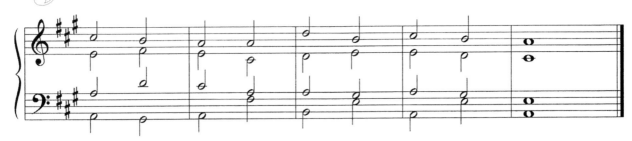

A:

Chords in Minor Keys

Harmonic Analysis:

Root Position Chords

in Minor Keys

In Chapter 9, we examined the typical chords in the major key. We stacked a third and fifth on each note of the major scale, adding sevenths to some chords and observed the qualities formed by the various intervallic patterns. In Chapter 10, we will explore typical chord qualities in the minor key.

The chords of the minor key are more variable than those of the major because while the major key has only one scale form, the minor scale form has three different versions, as we studied in Chapter 4. There is the natural, harmonic, and melodic minor, and each has a different scale.

Despite the variability of chord qualities in the minor key, the most typical chord formulations come through the use of the harmonic minor scale. Now we understand that the reason the natural minor scale with the raised seventh is called the "harmonic" minor is because it is that collection of notes that supplies the harmonies of minor key pieces. In fact, the harmonic minor scale is not really a scale at all but rather a pool of pitches that composers use to create the vertical, or chordal, aspect of music.

Example 10-1 reminds us of the d harmonic minor scale. You'll recall that in the harmonic minor, the natural minor scale is altered by raising the leading tone a half-step. Scale degree 7, "c," is raised a half-step to "c#."

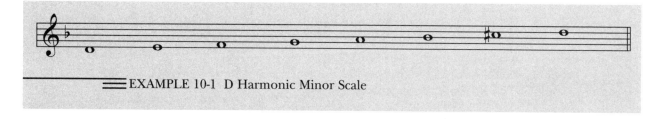

EXAMPLE 10-1 D Harmonic Minor Scale

With one exception, the triads and seventh chords are constructed out of the notes of the harmonic minor scale. Example 10-2 demonstrates the triads on each scale degree. Notice that scale degree 7 occurs in the V and vii° chords and that it is raised a half-step, the alteration that distinguishes the harmonic from the natural minor. The one exception to the use of pitches in the harmonic minor in building triads is in the III chord. Scale degree 7 is the fifth of the III chord and you'll notice that in that case "c" is not raised to "c#." The reason for the alteration in the V and vii° chords is that these chords typically resolve to i, and raising the 7 of the scale creates a strong gravitational pull to i. The reason scale degree 7 is not raised in the III chord is because III does *not* typically return to i, so there is no need to raise that note. Just as in the melodic minor ascending scale we raised scale degree 7 when returning to the tonic and lowered it when moving away from the tonic, the same principle may be observed with harmony. Chords with scale degree 7 that go to the tonic chord (V and vii°) in progressions get raised a half-step; the chord with scale degree 7 that does not go to i in progressions (III) does not get raised. Example 10-2 shows the intervallic content of each triad (the arrangement of major and minor thirds). Below each triad is the function of the chord from i to i. Note again that the roman numeral symbols indicate the triad qualities: upper case letters (III, V, VI) indicate major triads; lower case roman numerals indicate minor triads (i and iv), while the two diminished triads (ii° and vii°) are represented by lower case roman numerals with a circle to the upper right.

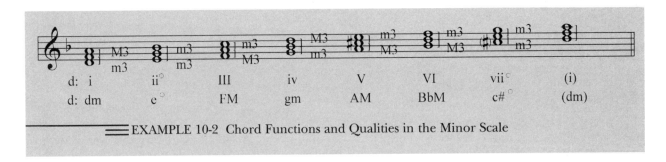

EXAMPLE 10-2 Chord Functions and Qualities in the Minor Scale

Again, we must be cognizant of the fact that there are three scale forms for minor keys and the melodic language of a piece will generate the harmonies. For example, the chord built on scale degree 4 is sometimes major and the chord built on scale degree 5 is sometimes minor. But the typical triads on each scale degree is as illustrated in Example 10-2. These chord qualities are listed below. **You should memorize them,** as that will save time when you do a harmonic analysis of a sequence of chords.

Minor chords of the minor scale: i, iv
Major chords of the minor scale: III, V, VI
Diminished chords of the minor scale: ii° and vii°

Note that there are only two qualities in common between the major and minor scales, V (which is typically major in both modes) and vii° (which is diminished in both modes). This helps account for the very different sound of the major and minor modes.

The procedure for writing harmonies in minor keys is the same as that observed in major keys. Composers string together chords, and the sequences that are produced are called progressions. Progressions gravitate toward a resolution on the i chord, which creates a sense of closure and finality, whether temporarily as at the end of a musical phrase or section, or with a sense of finality, as at the end of a movement or piece. You will learn more about harmonic progressions in Chapters 11 and 12.

Any triad may add a seventh in minor keys just as any triad may add a seventh in major keys. Example 10-3 demonstrates the seventh chord built on each degree of the scale, identifying the quality of the seventh to the right of the chord (major, minor, or diminished). The roman numeral symbol for the chord is indicated below it, and below that is the quality content of the chord. As with the major key, the first letter indicates the triad quality, the second letter indicates the interval between the root and seventh of the chord. For the sevenths built on scale degrees 2 and 7, the symbol is different. For ii, the diagonal line through the circle followed by a 7 indicates that the chord is a half diminished seventh, which means that it has a minor seventh between the root and the seventh of the chord. For vii°, the circle without the diagonal line followed by a 7 indicates that the chord is fully diminished, which means that there is a diminished seventh (nine half-steps) between the root and seventh. Whenever you see a circle (with or without the diagonal line), that's an indication of a diminished triad.

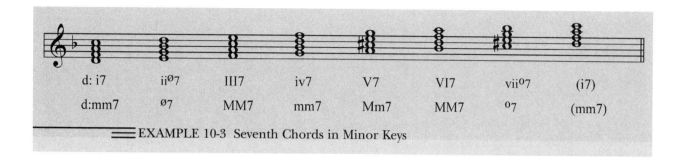

d: i7	ii°7	III7	iv7	V7	VI7	vii°7	(i7)
d:mm7	°7	MM7	mm7	Mm7	MM7	°7	(mm7)

EXAMPLE 10-3 Seventh Chords in Minor Keys

As discussed in the preceding chapter, sevenths are added to some chord functions more frequently than others. As in the major keys, V7 is by far the most frequent seventh chord in minor keys. The next most frequent (although far behind V7 in frequency) seventh chord is ii°7 followed by vii°7. (Note once again the difference between a fully diminished seventh chord and half diminished seventh chord. Both triads are diminished, but in the fully diminished seventh chord, there is a diminished seventh between the root and seventh. In the half diminished seventh chord, there is a minor seventh between the root and the seventh.) The other sevenths appear in classical tonal music (although i7 is rare) but with less frequency. The chart of triads and most frequent seventh chords is reproduced in Example 10-4. When you build your own scales and chords prior to doing a harmonic analysis, you should follow this model: i, III, iv, and VI will be written as triads. ii°7, V7, and vii°7 will be written as seventh chords.

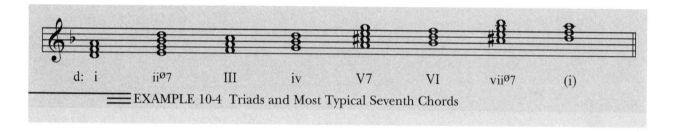

d: i	ii°7	III	iv	V7	VI	vii°7	(i)

EXAMPLE 10-4 Triads and Most Typical Seventh Chords

Now we can analyze a progression in a minor key. The procedure will be exactly the same as analyzing progressions in a major key. Note in Example 10-5 that the open position chords are first reduced to close position. The bass note serves as the point of reference and all other pitches except the doubled pitches are written as close as possible above the bass. Once the chords are reduced, they are checked against the functions (roman numerals) illustrated in Example 10-4. Note too that the symbol of upper or lower case, or lower case with the diminished circle symbol, coincides with the qualities we have learned to associate with these chords.

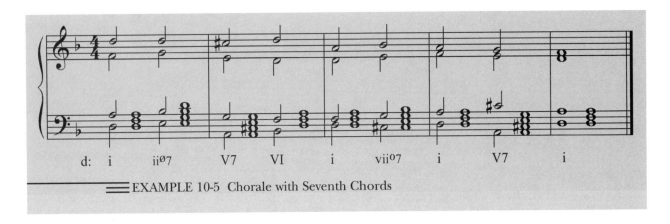

d: i   ii∅7   V7   VI   i   vii°7   i   V7   i

EXAMPLE 10-5 Chorale with Seventh Chords

Do a harmonic analysis of the chorale in Example 10-7. To do that, you'll need to construct the triads on i, III, iv, and VI, and seventh chords on ii°, V, and vii° for B minor in Example 10-6. Use Example 10-4 in D minor as a model. Note that **you must raise scale degree 7** in the V7 and vii°7 chords, which is the third of the V7 chord and the root of the vii°7 chord.

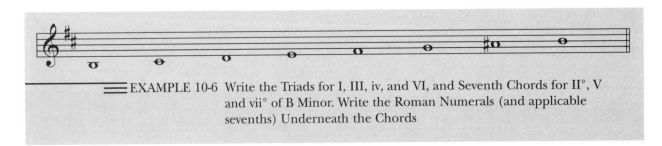

EXAMPLE 10-6 Write the Triads for I, III, iv, and VI, and Seventh Chords for II°, V and vii° of B Minor. Write the Roman Numerals (and applicable sevenths) Underneath the Chords

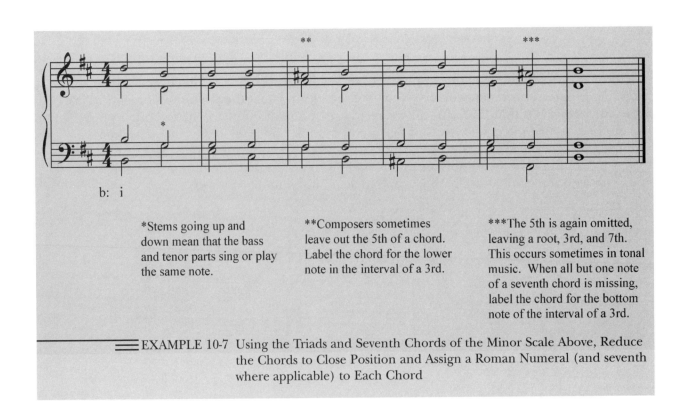

b: i

*Stems going up and down mean that the bass and tenor parts sing or play the same note.

**Composers sometimes leave out the 5th of a chord. Label the chord for the lower note in the interval of a 3rd.

***The 5th is again omitted, leaving a root, 3rd, and 7th. This occurs sometimes in tonal music. When all but one note of a seventh chord is missing, label the chord for the bottom note of the interval of a 3rd.

EXAMPLE 10-7 Using the Triads and Seventh Chords of the Minor Scale Above, Reduce the Chords to Close Position and Assign a Roman Numeral (and seventh where applicable) to Each Chord

Name: _____

Fill in the blanks for the questions below.

1) In a minor key, the notes that comprise the harmonies are most typically drawn from the _____ minor scale.

2) In a minor key, ____ and ____ are most typically minor triads.

3) In a minor key, ____, ____, and ____ are most typically major triads.

4) In a minor key, ____ and ____ are most typically diminished triads.

5) In a minor key, the three triads that contain scale degree 7 are ____, ____, and ____.

6) In a minor key, two of the three triads listed in question 5 that contain scale degree 7 typically raise that note a half step. The two triads that typically raise scale degree 7 are ____ and ____.

7) In a minor key, there is a m7 between the root and seventh of the ____, ____, ____, and ____ chords.

8) In a minor key, there is a M7 between the root and seventh of the ____ and ____ chords.

9) In a minor key, there is a d7 between the root and seventh of the ____ chord.

10) In a minor key, the three most common chords to add a seventh to the triad in tonal classical music are ____, ____, and ____.

11) Write the roman numeral symbols for the seven chords of the minor key. Add 7 for the chords built on the second, fifth, and seventh degrees of the scale.

_____ _____ _____ _____ _____ _____ _____

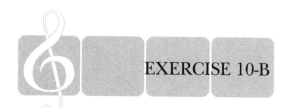

EXERCISE 10-B

Name: _____

For each exercise, on a seperate sheet of staff paper, write all the triads for i, III, iv, and VI and all the seventh chords on ii°, V, and vii° in the indicated keys and label each chord with roman numerals and 7 where applicable. Then reduce the open position chords in each exercise to close position and indicate the roman numerals. Add a 7 where necessary.

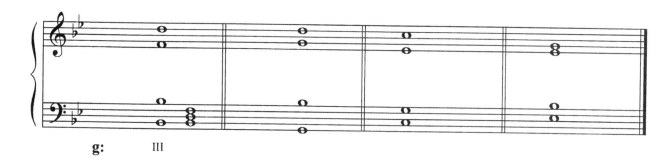

g: III

c:

f#:

a:

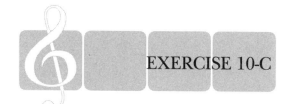

EXERCISE 10-C

Name: _____

For each exercise, on a seperate sheet of staff paper, write all the triads for i, III, iv, and VI
as well as seventh chords on ii°, V, and vii° in the indicated keys (as in Example 10-4) and label each
chord with roman numerals and sevenths where applicable. Then reduce the open position chords
in each exercise to close position and indicate the roman numerals.
Add a 7 to seventh chords.

f:

e:

g:

c#:

Inversions, Cadences, and Harmonic Analysis

In the previous two chapters, all of the sonorities we dealt with were in what is termed "root position." Chords are considered in **root position** when the root of the chord is in the bass voice. Root position chords are easy to recognize. Since chords are constructed in thirds, triads or seventh chords that contains only consecutive thirds in relationship to each other are in root position. The roman numerals for these chords refer to the roots of the chords.

Composers do not write every chord in root position, however, for two primary reasons. The first is that the bass line that results from progressions of root position chords leaps around quite a bit. Leaping bass lines are difficult to sing, and they prohibit the composition of a smoother and more melodic bass line. Take a look at Example 11-1. You'll notice that seven of the ten intervals in the bass are leaps rather than steps. Composers can write smoother bass lines by writing some chords with tones other than the root in the bass. The other primary reason for writing some chords with tones other than the root in the bass is for variety. Root position chords are very stable and solid. As we shall see, chords with tones other than the root in the bass have different sonorities and add dimension to the harmonic language of music. For both of the aforementioned reasons, composers may put any chord tone—root, third, fifth, or seventh—in the bass of a chord. In this chapter, we will learn how to name chords with tones other than the root in the bass.

b: i

EXAMPLE 11-1

To invert something is to change its order or position. When the order of tones in a chord is changed so that the root is no longer the bottom note, we call the new arrangement of tones an **inversion.** Any chord that does not have the root in the bass voice is regarded as **inverted. Inverted**

chords are typical in tonal music for the reasons listed above: (1) inverting chords gives greater flexibility to the bass line, which as a consequence can be smoother, and (2) the different sonorities of various inverted and root position chords create harmonic variety.

Any tone of a triad or seventh chord can be in the bass. Example 11-2 illustrates triads and seventh chords in all their possible inversions. Below the chords is a description of what member of the chord is in the bass. Above the chords is a the term for each chord. Notice that in the case of both the triad and the seventh chord, the only chord in each respective group in which the tones are stacked in thirds is the root position triad and root position seventh chord. You'll note too that the relative position of the notes to each other is changed in each of the inverted (non-root position) chords. The root is inverted (moved to the top of the stack) in the 1st inversion triad and 1st inversion seventh chord. The root and third are inverted (moved to the top of the stack) in the 2nd inversion triad and 2nd inversion seventh chord, and the root, third, and fifth are inverted (moved to the top of the stack) in the 3rd inversion seventh chord.

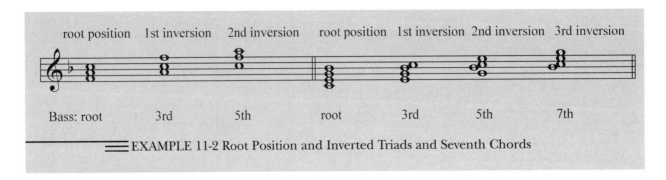

EXAMPLE 11-2 Root Position and Inverted Triads and Seventh Chords

Composers and theorists distinguish among root position chords and their various inversions by using arabic numerals. Inversions are indicated according to the intervals of the stacked notes above the bass note. The chords above are reproduced in Example 11-3, but now the intervals from the bass note is given under the chords in their order above the bass. For example, in a root position triad, the intervals above the bass are 5 and 3. The top note is a fifth above the bass, and the middle note is a third above the bass. These numbers change in the first inversion triad, which is labeled 6 and 3 above the bass as the top note is a sixth above the bass and the middle note is a third above the bass. The numbering system continues in that fashion for all of the chords. The seventh chord in root position is labeled 7, 5, 3 above the bass because the top note is a seventh above the root, the next note below is a fifth above the bass, and the note immediately above the bass note is a third. Look at each stack and observe the intervals above the bass notes. The bottom line indicates which note of the chord is in the bass.

root position	1st inversion	2nd inversion	root position	1st inversion	2nd inversion	3rd inversion
5	6	6	7	6	6	6
3	3	4	5	5	4	4
			3	3	3	2
Bass: root	3rd	5th	root	3rd	5th	7th

EXAMPLE 11-3 Root Position and Inverted Triads and Seventh Chords with Inversion Symbols

As we see, inversions are represented by a list of the intervallic content above the bass note. In earlier times, composers represented chords in a musical shorthand. Sometimes they would write just the bass note and write the inversion numerals below that, from which the performer would improvise the chords. (This practice has resurfaced in performances of Early Music.) Because there is much musical information that exists in a score and it is important to represent various indications as succinctly as possible, the cumbersome system of representing every note above the bass of a chord was stream-lined. The 5 and 3 of the root position triad was eliminated. Any triad without numbers is considered to be in root position. First inversion triads are represented by a 6 (the 3 is eliminated). Second inversion triads are represented by a 6 and 4. To distinguish it from a root position triad, the root position seventh chord is represented by a 7. The first inversion seventh chord is represented by the numerals 6 and 5. The second inversion seventh chord is represented by the numerals 4 and 3 (there is already a chord represented by a 6 and 4, the second inversion triad). The third inversion seventh chord is represented by the numbers 4 and 2. The chart from Example 11-3 is altered in Example 11-4 to illustrate the shorthand numbering system through which chords and inversions are represented.

root position	1st inversion	2nd inversion	root position	1st inversion	2nd inversion	3rd inversion
	6	6 4	7	6 5	4 3	4 2
Bass: root	3rd	5th	root	3rd	5th	7th

EXAMPLE 11-4 Triads and Inversions

When we describe a chord, we use the numerals above to indicate whether it is in root position or in inversion. Note that no two numeral sets are alike, which makes it possible to easily distinguish the position of the chords from each other.

The table in Example 11-5 succinctly lists the chords, their numeral symbols, what they are called (root position, first inversion, etc.) and what note will be found in the bass. **You should memorize this.** We have already learned the system of roman numerals that is used to describe the function of chords in a key. Now we see that the practice of harmonic analysis uses two different numerical systems to describe chords in the tonal context. The roman numerals describe the root of a given chord in relationship to the key center or tonic of the scale. The arabic numerals represent the position (root or inversion) of each chord. In the chart below, the V and V7 chords are used arbitrarily to represent chord function; this is followed by the arabic numerals (where applicable) that indicate the voicing of the chord (i.e. what chord tone is in the bass).

	Root Position	1st Inversion	2nd Inversion	3rd Inversion
Triad	V	V6	V6/4	——
Seventh Chord	V7	V6/5	V4/3	V4/2
Bass Note:	Root	3rd	5th	7th

EXAMPLE 11-5 Triad and Seventh Chords and Inversions

We now have the means to analyze root position and inverted chords in a tonal context. Example 11-7 illustrates four chords in the key of Bb Major. The first chord in each measure is the actual music. The chord or chords that follows are the steps the theorist takes to figure out what the root (and therefore the function) of the chord is and whether it is in root position or inversion. These chords are voiced in traditional four-part "chorale" style. The first step is to reduce the open position triads to close position as we did in our chapters dealing with root position chords. We do this in order to determine the root of the chord, without which we cannot name it or understand how it functions in a key. In Example 11-7a, when we reduce the open position triad to close position above the bass, we see that the three notes are stacked in thirds above the bass. Any chord in which tones are stacked in thirds above the bass is in root position. Now check the triads in Example 11-6 and determine that a root position triad built on "bb" is labeled I. Now check the chart in Example 11-5. A triad in which the root is in the bass is labeled solely by roman numeral. No arabic numerals need to be assigned as a roman numeral without arabic numerals means that the triad is in root position. In Example 11-7b, you'll notice that when the notes are all stacked in close position, the resulting chord is not in root position because it is not stacked in thirds; there is a second between the top two notes. In order to ascertain what the root of that chord is, the notes must be rearranged until they are all in thirds, stacked above the bass. The third chord in measure two restacks the chord so that it is all in thirds. The lowest note of a stack of thirds will always be the root. Now we know that the root of the chord in (b) is "c." Looking at Example 11-6, we see that a chord built on "c" is a ii chord. Since there is a seventh as well in the chord, we know it is a ii7. We then ask ourselves whether the root, third, fifth, or seventh is in the bass. "Eb" is the third of a "c" minor seventh chord. Now we check the chart in Example 11-5 and see that a seventh chord with the third in the bass is labeled 6/5. Therefore, we label this chord ii6/5, which means that the root of the chord is the second degree of the scale and that it has a seventh (a ii7 chord) and that it is in first inversion (which means that the third of the chord is in the bass). The procedure is the same for Example 11-6c. First we reduce the chord to close position above the bass. Noting that the chord is not in root position, we rearrange the notes until they are stacked in thirds above a bass note. That gives us the root, which is the bottom note. "F" is the root of that chord and it is a seventh chord because it has four notes. We check our chord functions in Example 11-6 and determine that a four-note chord built on "f" in Bb major is V7 in the key. Now we determine the inversion symbol, asking ourselves whether the root, third, fifth, or seventh is in the bass. It is the seventh, "eb," that is in the bass. Checking the chart in Example 11-5, we see that a chord with the seventh in the bass is labeled 4/2. Since the root is the fifth degree of the scale and the chord is in third inversion (seventh in the bass), we label it V4/2. We follow the same procedure in Example 11-7d. When stacking the notes in close position, we see that it is not in thirds. Restacking it, we discover that "bb" is the root. "Bb" is I in the key of Bb major. We then determine the inversion symbol by checking the chart in Example 11-5. A triad with the fifth in the bass is labeled 6/4, so this chord is labeled I6/4, which means that the root is the tonic of the scale (scale degree 1) and that it is in second inversion.

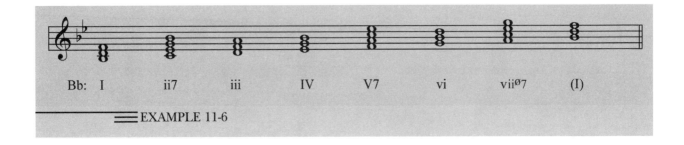

Bb: I   ii7   iii   IV   V7   vi   viiø7   (I)

EXAMPLE 11-6

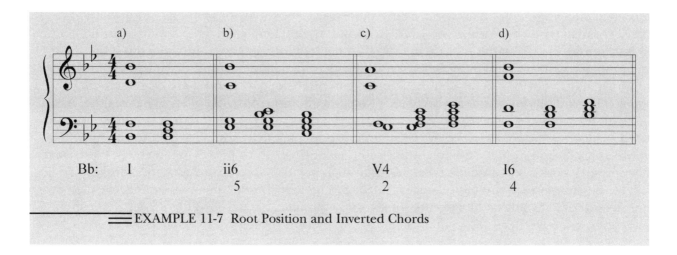

Bb: I   ii6   V4   I6
                     5   2   4

EXAMPLE 11-7 Root Position and Inverted Chords

Try this on your own. Example 11-8 gives you the notes of the D Minor scale; fill in the triads for i, III, iv, and VI, and the seventh chords for ii, V, and vii° (see Example 11-6 for a reminder of chord qualities if you've forgotten). Example 11-9 is a series of chords in D minor. Using the procedure outlined above, reduce the open position chords to close position, restack inverted chords to determine the root, and write the roman numeral of the chord and inversion symbol where applicable.

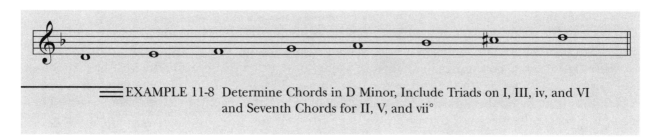

EXAMPLE 11-8 Determine Chords in D Minor, Include Triads on I, III, iv, and VI and Seventh Chords for II, V, and vii°

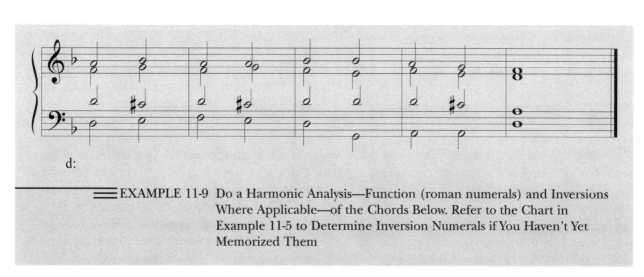

d:

EXAMPLE 11-9 Do a Harmonic Analysis—Function (roman numerals) and Inversions Where Applicable—of the Chords Below. Refer to the Chart in Example 11-5 to Determine Inversion Numerals if You Haven't Yet Memorized Them

The harmonic analysis exercises in this and the previous chapter have been designed for the beginning student. To simplify the task as one learns to recognize and identify the chords and their function, only chord tones are used. While the texture of some music is chordal, with block chords defining the harmonies, much music is not. Harmony in polyphonic music is the result of two or more melodic lines rather than obvious chord units. Many types of homophonic music do not use block chords. In much keyboard music, for example, accompanimental figures in the bass do not outline the entire chord. Harmonies are produced in tandem with a melody line, which is often scalar rather than triadic. In most music, chords must be identified in the context of groups of notes, some of which may not belong to the chord. Notes that do not belong to a chord are called **non-chord tones.** They enliven the harmonic language by creating tension. Also, melodies in music often have a large number of steps, while chords tones are always a third apart. As the student becomes more practiced in hearing harmonies, he or she becomes more adept at determining which notes belong to a chord and which do not. In addition, music often **modulates,** which means that it changes keys, and hearing such changes and labeling the chords in such passages correctly takes a good deal of practice. But for our purposes in this basic course, understanding that chords cohere in sequences called progressions and being able to identify the roman numeral function, as well as identifying and naming inversions, is an excellent step in understanding how chords relate to each other in tonal music.

Cadences

Cadences are harmonic formulas that accompany points of rest at the ends of phrases, sections, movements, or pieces. Typically, a cadence is a point of rest, either momentary or final. Example 11-10 is an excerpt from a work for piano by Muzio Clementi (1752–1832), his Sonatina, Opus 36, No. 5, second movement. The texture of the music is in typical keyboard style. The melody is on the top staff, and the homophonic accompaniment, containing some of the chord tones, is on the bottom staff. To do a harmonic analysis, the student must disregard some of the pitches, like the "a" and "f#" in measure 4. Nevertheless, the music clearly alternates mostly between tonic and (I) dominant (V) chords. This excerpt breaks down neatly into two four-measure phrases. The second four-measure phrase begins like the first, except that it starts up a major second, starting on "a" instead of "g."

Although there is no significant change in the texture, nor a pause in the melody line, the listener hears that measure 4 is the end of the first phrase. This is reinforced by what appears to be a repetition of the beginning of that phrase starting on "a" on the second beat of that measure. The second phrase concludes on the downbeat of measure 8. If you play this for yourself or listen to a recording, you will notice that the harmony on the first beat of measure 4 sounds inconclusive, while the harmony on the first beat of measure 8 is more conclusive. This is because the chord implied on the downbeat of measure 4 is a V chord, which is heard as such even though the third of the chord is missing. Since only a return to I creates a sense of resolution, the effect of the V chord is that the harmonic progression is incomplete. The downbeat of measure 8 returns to a I chord, although it is in first inversion, preceded by a V7 chord that is missing the third. The harmonic progression is closed, and while there is not the same sense of finality as there would be were that I6 chord a I, the phrase does seem closed because of the return to the tonic harmony. (At the same time, the use of I6 causes just enough instability to cause the movement to seem like it needs to go on. As this is only the beginning of the movement, such a lack of finality is appropriate.) The two cadence points, in measure 3 and the downbeat of measure 4, and in measure 7 and the downbeat of measure 8, are marked with brackets. You'll notice that the first measure is not complete; it contains one beat rather than two. When music begins without a full measure, the music contained is called a **pickup,** and the measure is called a **pickup measure.** A more formal word for a pickup that does not occur on the beat is **anacrusis.** You'll notice that in addition to notes and rhythms, a **dynamic marking** (related to volume and attack) is also indicated, p for piano, or soft. In addition, there are indications called articulation markings, which are the composer's instructions to the performer about how to play the music. The curved lines connecting groups of notes are called **slurs,** which instruct the performer to play the notes in a smooth and connected way. The periods under the music in the left hand and in measures 3 and 6 are called **staccato** marks and indicate to the performer that a note should be played for half of its value. Much of the character of music is determined by dynamics and articulation marks.

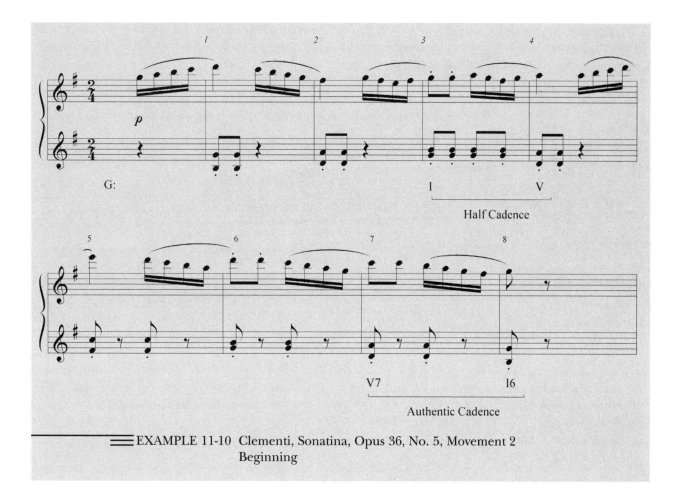

EXAMPLE 11-10 Clementi, Sonatina, Opus 36, No. 5, Movement 2
Beginning

These formulae, I-V and V-I(6), are typical cadences. There are four cadence types that we will learn. Two of these cadence types are inconclusive, that is, they do not bring the harmonic dimension of a phrase or section to a place of rest. That is because in both of these cadences, the final chord is not I. In the case of the **half cadence**, the usual temporary resting place is on V, although on occasion the music pauses on IV (or iv in a minor key). This is the only cadence that doesn't rely on a sequence of two chords, and the chord preceding V may be anything. For our purposes, we'll display the preceding chord as IV, but it doesn't matter what it is. What is most important is that the music pauses and the melodic phrase ends on a V chord.

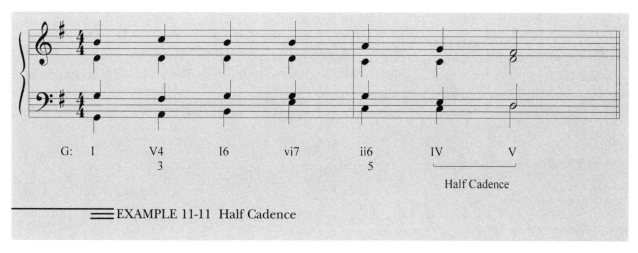

EXAMPLE 11-11 Half Cadence

The other inconclusive cadence is called the **deceptive cadence**, aptly named because instead of progressing from V or V7 to I (or i), as one would expect, the final chord is something other than I, in most cases vi (or VI in minor keys). Since there is no sense of harmonic rest in either of these cadences, the music must continue in order to create a sense of closure.

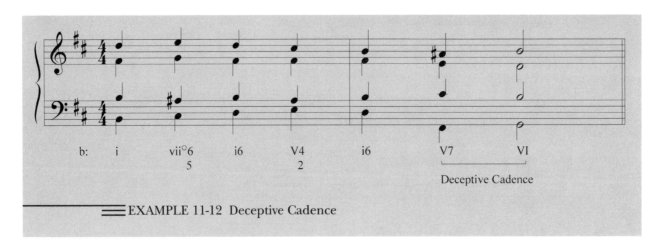

EXAMPLE 11-12 Deceptive Cadence

Two cadences are conclusive, which is to say that they create a sense of harmonic closure at the end of a phrase, section, movement, or piece. By far the most frequent of these cadences is the **authentic cadence**, which progresses from V or V7 to I (or i in minor keys). (The vii°(7) chord may be substituted for V or V7, with similar effect).

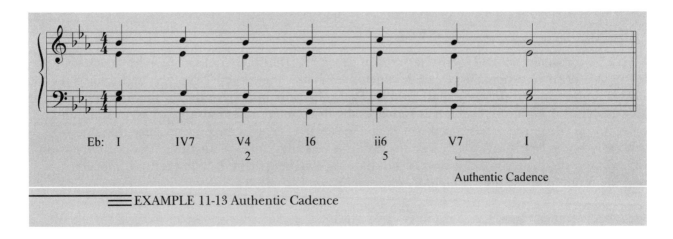

EXAMPLE 11-13 Authentic Cadence

The other conclusive cadence is called a **plagal cadence,** sometimes known as the "amen" cadence for its role in ecclesiastical music. This progression goes from IV-I, and often accompanies the word "amen" in music of the Christian church.

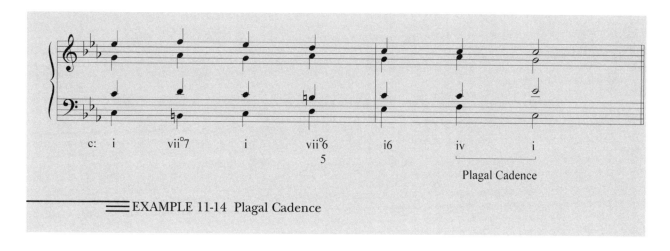

c: i   vii°7   i   vii°$^6_5$ i6   iv   i

Plagal Cadence

EXAMPLE 11-14 Plagal Cadence

Memorize the formulae for the four cadences we've learned.

CADENCES

Inconclusive Cadences

	Harmonic Formula
Half Cadence	**(I)–V (or less frequently, IV) (preceding chord is variable)**
Deceptive Cadence	**V(7)–VI (vii°(7)) may substitute for V or V7**

Conclusive Cadences

	Harmonic Formula
Authentic Cadence	**V(7)–I**
Plagal Cadence	**IV–I**

For the cadences above, chords in the minor key are substituted in minor key cadences.

Name: _____

Fill in the blanks for the questions below.

1) A triad in first inversion is labeled _____.

2) A triad in second inversion is labeled _____.

3) A seventh chord in root position is labeled _____.

4) A seventh chord in first inversion is labeled _____.

5) A seventh chord in second inversion is labeled _____.

6) A seventh chord in third inversion is labeled _____.

7) A first inversion triad has the _____ in the bass.

8) A second inversion triad has the _____ in the bass.

9) A first inversion seventh chord has the _____ in the bass.

10) A second inversion seventh chord has the _____ in the bass.

11) A third inversion seventh chord has the _____ in the bass.

12) A **half cadence** typically consists of _____ _____.

13) A **deceptive cadence** typically consists of _____ _____.

Name: _____

14) An **authentic cadence** typically consists of _____ _____.

15) A **plagal cadence** consists of _____ _____.

EXERCISE 11-B

Name: _____

Reduce the following chords to close position. Restack the chord in thirds where necessary.
For each chord, write root position when the root is in the bass, "1st inversion" when the third is in the bass,
"2nd inversion" when the fifth is in the bass, and " 3rd inversion" when the seventh is in the bass. Beneath that,
write whether the chord is a triad or a seventh chord.

1st inversion
seventh chord

Follow the same procedure as above, now using roman numerals
and inversion symbols to identify the chords.

A: I6

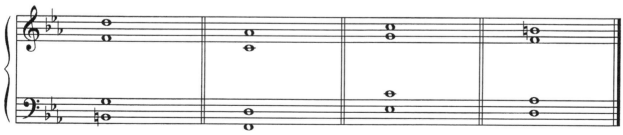

c:

EXERCISE 11-C

Name: _____

The following examples are in C Major and g Minor. Each example is six measures long. On a separate sheet of staff paper, construct the chords for both keys. Reduce the open position chords to close position and determine the roman numeral and inversion symbols where applicable. (Refer to Example 11-5 if you haven't yet memorized the symbols for root position seventh chords and inversions.)

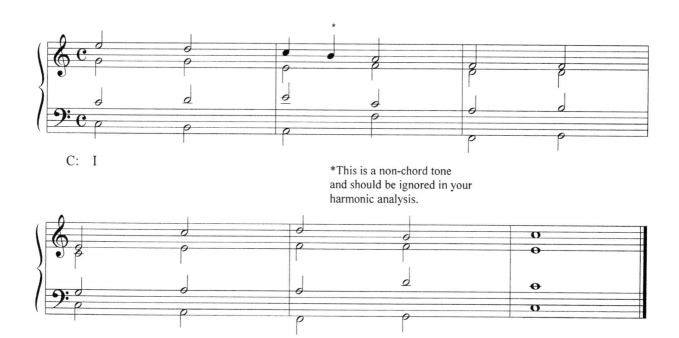

C: I

*This is a non-chord tone
and should be ignored in your
harmonic analysis.

g: i

EXERCISE 11-D

Name: _____

Do a harmonic analysis of all of the chords and then, considering the last two chords in each exercise, indicate the cadence (authentic, plagal, half, or deceptive).

C:

e:

D:

f#:

E:

g#:

Final Composition

We've learned to read notes and rhythms, identify keys, intervals, and chords, and compose melodies. The concluding project is to put all of these skills to work in a creative way through the composition of a twenty-four measure piece. To do this, we will build on previous assignments, accompanying the two melodies, major and minor, written in Chapters 6 and 7 with typical classical music progressions. Examples 12-1 and 12-2 illustrate typical progressions in tonal music in major and minor keys. Although the reality of chord progressions is more varied and complex than the simplified chart below, the beginning composer will find this reduction of principal tendencies in progressions helpful. Although the progression possibilities shown below are not carved in stone, they do describe the most typical tendencies of chords in tonal progressions. Arrows illustrate how chords progress. Avoid moving from chord to chord where no arrow demonstrates a progression.

The charts below break chord functions down into three basic types: tonic, pre-dominant, and dominant. We will use these charts as guidelines for writing progressions to accompany our major and minor key melodies.

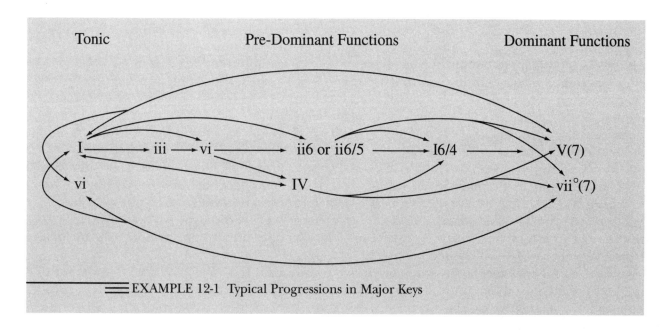

EXAMPLE 12-1 Typical Progressions in Major Keys

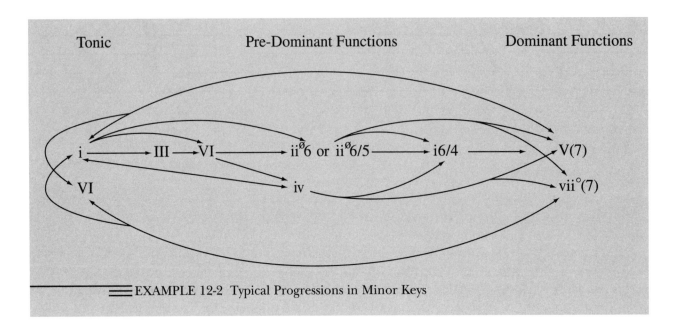

| Tonic | Pre-Dominant Functions | Dominant Functions |

EXAMPLE 12-2 Typical Progressions in Minor Keys

The chord built on the third degree of the major scale occurs in minor keys but is not very common in major keys. When used at all in the latter, it generally precedes the vi chord. The strongest root motion from chord to chord in tonal music is that between chords a perfect fifth apart. V-I (or i in minor) is a root progression of a perfect fifth: the root of the V chord is a perfect fifth above the root of the I chord. (All generalizations in this section apply to chords in the minor key as well). Similarly, the root of the ii chord is a perfect fifth above the root of a V chord. Moving backwards (from right to left on our chart), the root of the vi chord is a perfect fifth above the root of the ii chord, and the root of the iii chord is a fifth above the root of the vi chord. Root motion of a descending perfect fifth creates a very strong progression. Most important is the root motion of a perfect fifth between the V(7) and I chords, and there is quite a bit of variability in the chords that precede the authentic cadence. Note in the chart above that the I chord can be followed by any chord. The "skeleton" progression, which may be fleshed out with other chords, goes from tonic to predominant to dominant back to tonic. V(7) or its substitute, vii°(7) is the penultimate chord, and the tonality defining chord. Once the V(7) is reached, the strong expectation of a return to tonic is created. This is what makes the vi chord so effective as a deceptive cadence in motion. The listener expects I but hears vi instead. Note that the arrow from the dominant functions head back to tonic, where they either reach it in most cases, or substitute vi for tonic. Note too that the most frequent predominant chord, ii6 (ii is a chord most frequently found in first inversion), almost always proceeds to V(7), sometimes through I6/4 and most often directly. The I6/4 chord is used at the cadence, preceding the V(7). Called a cadential I6/4, it most frequently occurs on a strong beat, usually the first beat of a measure, and resolves to V(7) on a weak beat.

As you accompany your major and minor key melodies with chords, you will want to refer to the chart of typical progressions. To provide an example of how to set your melodies, the melodies from Chapters 6 and 7 will be used as models.

When setting melodies, chords are used that are **consonant** (creating agreeable sounds) with the notes of the melody. Put most simply, chords should be used that have as many notes in common with the melody. To be able to visualize this, it might be helpful to start with the scales of the keys of the piece and number them. The numbers represent the scale degrees of the notes.

The major key melody in Chapter 6 is in G Major. When setting out to accompany the melody with chords, we first represent all the chords of the key with their roman numeral functions listed below. In addition, all of the notes are numbered by scale degrees. The tonic triad contains scale degrees 1, 3, and 5 and are numbered accordingly, while the chord built on the second degree (the supertonic) contains scale degrees 2, 4, 6, and 1 (the added pitch is the seventh of the chord, which we include on chords ii, V, and vii°).

Example 12-3 sets out the G major scale with roman numeral designations below and each scale degree numbered to the right of the chords.

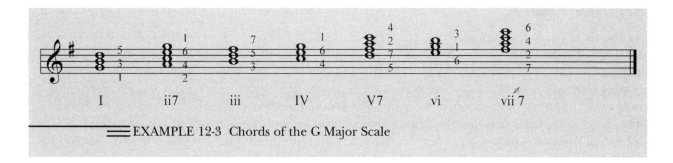

EXAMPLE 12-3 Chords of the G Major Scale

The major key melody in G major is now reintroduced. The numbers above the notes describe the scale degrees. The notes below the staff are the measure numbers. The notes of the first measure—3, 5, 2, 2, and 3—are the third, fifth, second, second, and third degrees of the scale respectively. Once we know what scale degrees are in the chords and what scale degrees are in the melody, it will be easy to see which chords match appropriately with the melody notes.

EXAMPLE 12-4

In most of our exercises in the previous chapters, all of the notes in the exercises belonged to chords. But as we saw in the last chapter, melodies often contain non-chord tones, especially because melodies typically have many seconds, and chords are built on thirds. As we set our melodies, we will be aware that not every note will be part of a chord. What we are looking for are groups of notes that mostly comprise chords. There are several rules of thumb when determining what notes of a melody should be considered primary and which secondary. Rhythm plays a great role in determining what chord to use to accompany a melody. Notes on strong beats are taken more into account than notes on weak beats. Secondly, melodies with patterns of scale steps have a chord tone every other note. For example, if a scale pattern of 1-2-3 appears in a melody, 1 and 3 will be part of a chord while 2 will not be part of that chord. The composer would accompany that part of the melody with a chord that contains scale degrees 1 and 3 rather than 2. In cases where there are four scale steps, say 1-2-3-4, the determination of whether to accompany that melodic fragment with chords with 1 and 3 or 2 and 4 will depend in part on the progression desired, in part on which of those notes fall on stronger beats or parts of beats, and in part on what sounds most appropriate. For that reason, it is necessary to do the work of accompanying a melody at the piano or other chord instrument so that you will be guided by your ear.

Harmonic Rhythm

Harmonic rhythm is the speed at which the chords change in a piece or section of a piece. In much tonal music, harmonic rhythm becomes somewhat regularized, that is, most of the chords change at the same rate. For example, in chorales (hymns that are accompanied with chords), the harmonies change on every quarter note beat. In piano sonatas of Mozart, the chords often change once every half note. This is not a rule, and Mozart changes harmonic rhythms to suit his needs, often increasing the harmonic rhythm at the cadences or slowing down the harmonic rhythm when necessary. But many pieces do get into a harmonic rhythm that is fairly regular despite disruptions of the pattern. For our purposes, it is best to decide on a harmonic rhythm on the basis of the notes of the melody. You might strive to write two chords per measure (one on every half note in 4/4 time) and adjust that harmonic rhythm where necessary, especially at cadences.

As you prepare to set your major melody to chords, it will be useful to have the chart of typical progressions (Example 12-1), your scale and chords, with roman numerals below and scale degrees to the side of each chord (like Example 12-3) and your melody, with scale degrees marked above the melody notes. (You might copy 12-3 so that you can refer to it easily as you work.) Example 12-5 reproduces the chart of typical progressions, the major scale with roman numerals and scale degrees, and the melody.

Typical Tonal Progression in Major Keys

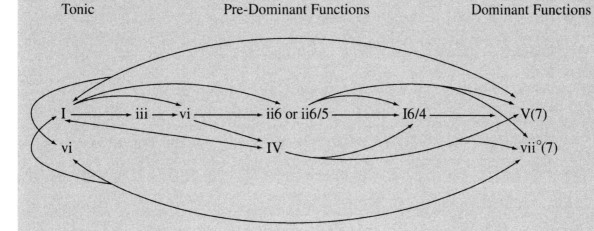

Tonic   Pre-Dominant Functions   Dominant Functions

G Major Scale with Roman Numerals and Scale Degrees

Setting a Major Key Melody

EXAMPLE 12-5 Typical Tonal Progressions in Major Keys

Now we have everything we need to set our melody. Once we establish the chords to be used with the melody notes, we are going to use an accompanimental figure to make the expression of those chords more musical. In the template below, you'll note that there are three lines per system. The top line is where the melody will be written. The middle line (which is the bottom line of the piano grand staff) is where the accompaniment will eventually be written. The bottom line is where you will put your block chords prior to expanding those chords into accompaniment figures. (This bottom line is a convenience for students to determine what chords to use and would not be found in piano music.) Example 12-6 sets the melody.

The basic harmonic rhythm of the piece will be one chord for every half note beat, or two per measure. The first thing to bear in mind as you begin to set your melody with chords is that composers often establish the tonic chord at the beginning of the melody, and you were encouraged to do so when you wrote your melodies. You were also encouraged to avoid the tonic at the end of measure 4 so that the music would be unresolved and wanting to push forward. As we know from our discussion of cadences, the half cadence is inconclusive, and that might be an appropriate choice if possible in measure 4 to create the need to move on harmonically. If you ended measure 4 on scale degree 5, 7, or 2, you will be able to write a half cadence (V) chord at the end of that measure. As measure 5 often emulates measure 1, the chords used in measure 5 may be the same as those in measure 1. If you have established tonic in measure 1, the repeat of I in measure 5 will be appropriate. The piece should end on the tonic chord. These chord choices set a harmonic frame around your melody, and then you may set about to fill in the details.

Using the principles above, we set the major key melody. As we do so, we bear in mind three principles. The first is that the scale degrees (represented by numbers) of the melody and chords coincide. Notes of the melody must appear in the chords for the whole to sound harmonious. Secondly, we make sure that the progressions formed by the sequence of chords follows the permissible progressions found in our chart of typical progressions. Finally, we avoid too much repetition of the same chords by substituting chords of the same category (tonic, pre-dominant, and dominant) where possible to create variety.

Let's apply these principles to the melody as set below. First, there is a correspondence between every group of melody notes and the chord chosen to accompany it. If you look through the example, you will discover that there is always at least one melody note in the chord. How do we make chord choices? Looking at the first measure (measures are numbered below the bass clef staff), we see that scale degrees 3 and 5 are accompanied by a I chord. There were two possible choices here: the I chord and the iii chord, both of which contain scale degrees 3 and 5. But iii in a major key is an atypical chord, and melodies often establish tonic at the outset. The tonality of G major is established by setting the first few notes of the melody with the tonic triad. The notes of the melody in the second half of measure 1 are scale degrees 2 and 3. The primary note is scale degree 2, which occurs twice in the melody and both times on the downbeat (the beginning of the beat). There are three chords with scale degree 2. They are ii, V, and vii°. Your choice here will depend on your ear and on where the progression continues. A V(7) or vii° chord tends to go to I (or vi). But the most important melody note of the first two beats of measure 2 is scale degree 4, and that is not in the tonic or vi chord. So neither V(7) nor vii° is a good choice for the second half of measure 1. That leaves ii as the chord of choice in the second half of measure 1. (In this way, we make certain that the chords we choose follow the correct tendencies of progressions.) We proceed in just this way, primarily making sure the chords selected match the notes of the melody, using our ears to determine what is the best choice of harmonies when there is a choice of more than one chord, and making sure that the progressions outlined in our chart of typical progressions are observed. Looking forward as you choose your chords will guide you in deciding which chords to use. There is also variety in the choices of chords used. All chords in a category can be substituted for any other. In the predominant category, either ii or IV may be used. In the dominant category, vii° may be substituted for V or V7 (although final cadences are best expressed with V or V7). vi may substitute for I after V, as a deceptive motion. In addition, chords within a category may be strung together, like ii-IV, or vii°-V(7). The harmonic setting in Example 12-6 has both consistency and variety. Note too that the harmonic rhythm is fairly steady but varied to create interest. In measures 1–3 and 5, there are two chords per measure. At both cadence points, measures 4 and 8, there is a faster harmonic rhythm. Use your ear to determine an attractive harmonic rhythm for your piece. Note that the completed setting has the melody labeled by scale degree, measure numbers beneath the piano bass part, chords labeled by scale degrees, and a roman numeral analysis beneath the "Block Chord" line. After setting the minor key melody, there will be a discussion of how to set the block chords in appropriate accompanimental style.

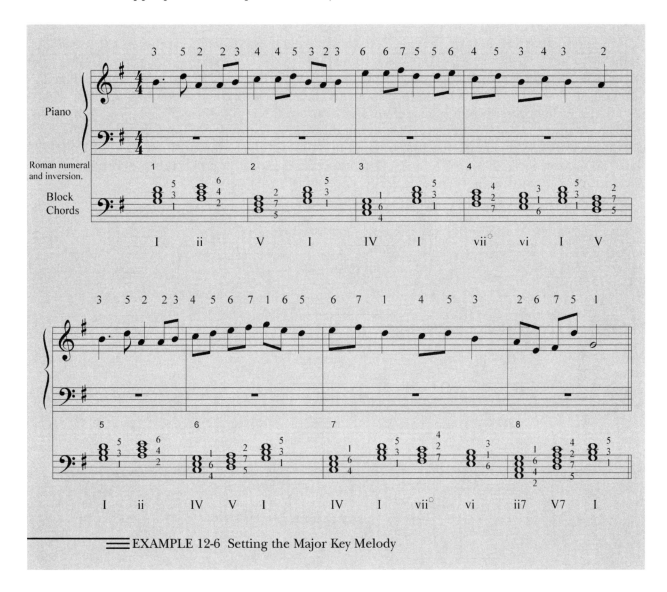

EXAMPLE 12-6 Setting the Major Key Melody

SETTING A MINOR KEY MELODY

The setting of the 8-measure major key melody constitutes the A section of our 24 measure piece that will be structured in A-B-A form. The B section will be a setting of the minor key melody, after which a return to the A section will round out the 24 measure form.

All of the advice accompanying the setting of a major key melody applies to the setting of the minor key melody, although there are other considerations when dealing with a minor key. Chords progress the same way they do in the major key, although the chord qualities reflect the minor rather than major key. The other change is that the composer must be mindful of the raised seventh degree in the chords. If we write the scale and associated chord tones, and raise the seventh in the V and vii° chords and then reproduce them in our melody setting, we will correctly write the appropriate chords. Remember that whether V goes to i or VI, the third of the V chord will be raised to make a major chord that "leans" to the resolution chord. The same is the case with the vii° chord. The root of that chord, the seventh degree of the scale, must be raised by half-step.

We now reproduce the melody from Chapter 7 and will use it for our B section. It was composed in e minor, the relative minor of G Major, so that it would work well with the A section. Sections in relative or parallel major and minor are compatible. They share common characteristics but provide different tonal colors.

You'll note that wherever there is a vii° or V chord, the seventh degree of the scale is raised from "d" to "d#." This creates a strong gravitational pull to the tonic or to the third of the VI chord. The vii° and V chords appearing in measures 1, 4, 5, 6, and 8 all have a "d#" rather than a "d" natural. The chords were chosen to accompany the melody on the basis of their appropriateness to the scale degrees used in the melody and in appreciation of typical progressions in tonal music. i progresses to vii°7 in measure 1, to Vi in measure two. Chords within a category (tonic, pre-dominant, and dominant) may follow each other and vii°7 goes to i or VI. Measures 3 and 4 have the progression iv, i, iv, i, V. A look at Example 12-2 demonstrates that this progression of chords is consistent with the chart of typical progressions.

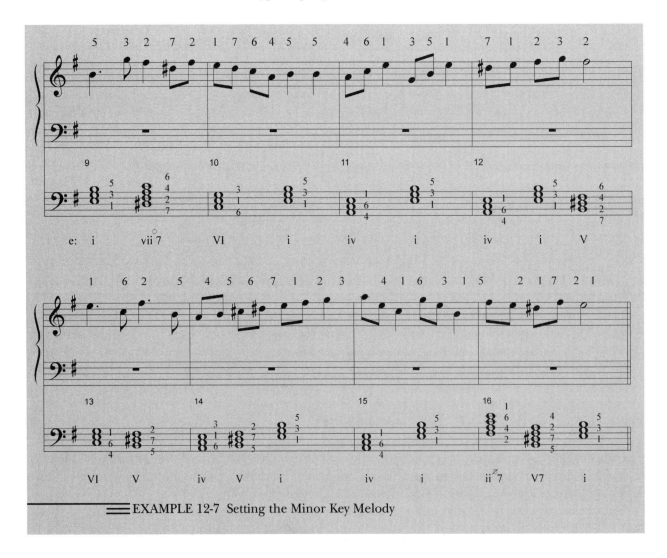

EXAMPLE 12-7 Setting the Minor Key Melody

Although block chords are used in some musical settings, an unrelenting string of block chords in the accompaniment becomes heavy and tedious. In addition, all of the chords above are in root position. This prevents the bass line from having a melodic profile and creates a redundant solidity in the sonority of the chords. A judicious mixing of root position chords and inversions will make the bass line more interesting and create variety in the effect of the sonority of the chords. Root position chords are very solid and stable, first inversion chords are less stable, and second and third inversion chords are very unstable. Because second inversion triads are used in restricted ways in tonal music, it is better for the beginning student to avoid them. The one exception is the cadential I6/4 chord, which may be used at a cadence and must be followed by a V or V7 chord. It must also occur on a strong beat and resolve to V(7) on a weak beat, and all voices that move must move down by step or half-step.

The next step is to choose inversions for some of the chords. First inversion is always allowed. In addition, the chords should be converted to an accompanimental pattern. You will find some possibilities at the end of the chapter. Note that the block chords and roman numerals in this next stage have been changed. Now there are inversions to create variety in the chord sonorities and to produce a more interesting bass line.

You will notice in the accompaniment figures below (Example 12-8) that there is a fair amount of variety. Composers often strive to make their accompaniments aesthetically pleasing and to find the right inflections to support the melody. You can experiment with different accompaniments, although it's best to create some consistency in the use of accompaniment figures. In the accompaniment below, the chords have been broken in several measures into a bass note and a chord. If you choose this kind of accompaniment, you can be flexible about how you voice the notes. Consider all of the notes in the treble and bass when deciding on what notes to use in the piano's left hand. Writing the upper notes of the accompaniment in open position keeps the bass from sounding too heavy. Note in the first measure in Example 12-8 that the bass note is a single note and that the other two notes of the chord are played in eighth notes, in open position, above it. The ii6 chord has the third of the chord in the bass and the other two members of the chord above it. All members of the chord are played in the left hand. In measure 4, however, the first chord is a vii°, but all the notes are not in the bass. The third chord member is in the soprano. This is acceptable, since all notes of the chord are present. You may omit the fifth of any chord that isn't diminished. The best tool for choosing chord inversions and an accompaniment is your ear.

Dynamics and Articulation

Dynamics refer to the volume of the music. The two main Italian terms for volume are *forte,* which means "strong" and *piano,* which means "soft." Thus the abbreviation for forte, a single f, is used to indicate that the music is to be played or sung loudly, while the single p tells the performer to perform the music softly. The word "**mezzo,**" which means "moderately," is used to modify piano and forte, making the piano a little louder and the forte a little softer. We also add p's or f's to indicate softer and louder. The chart below shows the gradations from softest to loudest.

ppp	*pp*	*p*	*mp*	*mf*	*f*	*ff*	*fff*
pianississimo	pianissimo	piano	mezzo-piano	mezzo-forte	forte	fortissimo	fortississimo
very, very soft	very soft	soft	mod. soft	mod. loud	loud	very loud	very, very loud

In addition, composers use crescendo and decrescendo marks, as seen in measures three and four in Example 12-8, below. The hairpin that gets wider (measure 3) is called a **crescendo**, and tells the performer to get gradually louder. The hairpin that gets narrower (measure 4) is called a **decrescendo**, and tells the performer to get gradually softer. Usually there is a dynamic marking at the end of a crescendo or decrescendo so that the performer knows how loud or soft to become.

Articulations tell musicians how to shape phrases and attack the notes. Slurs tell the performer to make no separation between the notes, which creates a smooth line. **Staccato** marks, which look like periods, tell the performer to make the note short, about one-half its usual value. (See measures 4 in the bass and 8 in the treble for examples.) Another useful marking is the accent (see the second and fourth beats of measure 7 below). This tells the performer to play that note louder than the surrounding ones.

Example 12-8 shows the finished composition. A is the setting of the major key melody, B is the setting of the minor key melody, and the A-B-A form is rounded by the return of the A, which is copied verbatim. In both A and B sections, the root position chords on the bottom line have been changed to include some inversions and the roman numeral altered to reflect those changes. (Note in measure 13 there is a second inversion triad on i. This is acceptable when that bass note passes between the two surrounding bass notes a third apart.) The block chords have been transformed into accompaniment figures. In the A section, we have a bass note and chords alternating, as well as block chords. In B, an **alberti bass** is used, which is a smooth, eighth note representation of the chords, alternating bass with members of the chords. Block chords are also used. Finally, dynamic markings and articulations have been added to give the music more shape. You now have a model for your own final composition. When the piece is performed, only the top two lines will be played.

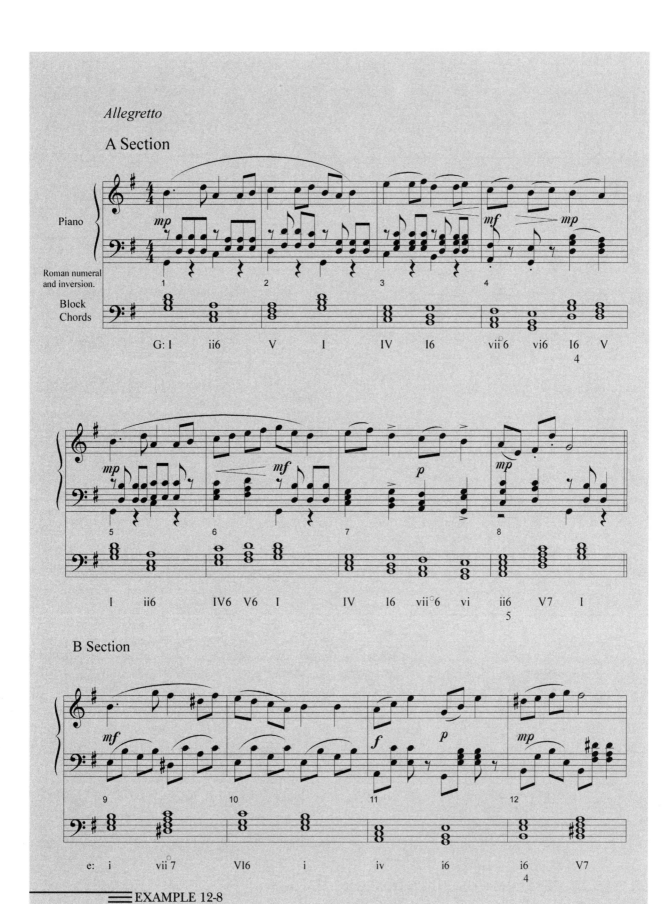

EXAMPLE 12-8

VI   i6   iv   V   i   iv6   i   ii°6 V7 i
      4   5

A Section (repeat of original A--it is not necessary to reproduce block chords and roman numerals.)

═══EXAMPLE 12-8 CONTINUED

Accompaniment Figures

The model composition above contains all the accompaniment figures that you'll need for your composition. There are three basic types used. They are reproduced below, showing different versions of a similar two-chord progression. Notice with the "oom-pah" or "oom-pah-pah-pah" bass that a single bass note is followed by notes from the chord, generally distributed in open position to produce a lighter sonority than a close position chord in the lower register. The "alberti" bass has less differentiation between the bass voice and chords, and presents the members of the chord one by one. Block chords, and a bass note with other chord members written above, are also viable. You may use any or all of these accompaniment figures as appropriate for your composition. Avoid writing block chords in close position below an octave below middle "c." This produces a muddy sound.

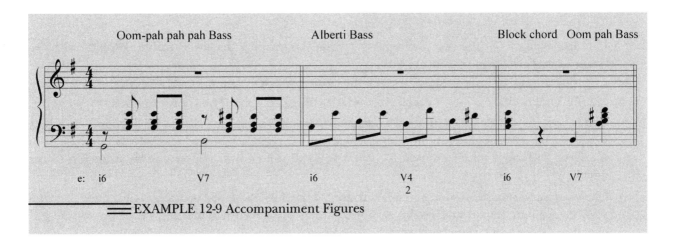

EXAMPLE 12-9 Accompaniment Figures

You are now ready to compose your own composition. Follow the instructions below. Exercise 12-A gives you the template for your final composition.

FINAL PROJECT INSTRUCTIONS

Your final project is to write a short composition for solo piano. The piece will demonstrate your knowledge of music: the ability to use many of the concepts you've learned in the previous chapters, especially about rhythm, melody, keys, and chords. The form of the piece should be as follows:

A	B	A(')
8 measures	8 measures	8 measures

Transfer the major key melodies you wrote in Chapters 6 and 7 to the upper line of each system. The major key melody will go in the A section, and the minor key melody in the B section. (When you are completely finished setting your melodies, copy the A section into measures 17–24 on the second page). The meter signature will go on the treble and bass of the first system. The key signature will go on all of the lines throughout the piece. You will need to sit at a piano or other instrument to do this work. Start by (1) accompanying your melody with block chords, indicated on the lowest staff of each three-staff system. (2) Next, assign a roman numeral to each of the chords, in the place indicated below the bottom staff. These chords are not to be played by the performer, but will help you figure out what pitches to use in your accompaniment. (3) Once you've written your block chords and roman numerals, reconsider these chords and use first inversion chords or cadential second inversion I6/4 triads to create variety and a smooth bass line where possible.

(4) Choose your accompaniment figures from those suggested in Example 12-9, or compose your own. Convert the block chords to accompanimental figures, and fill in the middle line, which is the left hand of the piano. (5) Add dymanic markings and articulations to give the music further shape. Give a basic direction about tempo or character at the beginning of your piece. Choose from among those listed below:

Grave: very slow and solemn
Largo: very slow and expressive
Andante: moderate "walking" speed
Moderato: moderate tempo
Allegretto: moderately fast
Allegro: fast
Presto: very fast

Here are some additional hints to consider:

- **Line up the beats of the two piano parts so that the music in bass and treble coincide with the beats. It is difficult to read otherwise.**

- **Confine the music to the places where the instrument sounds best. For example, don't have the piano play close position block chords in its lower register. The sound that results is muddy.**

- **When you do the Roman numeral analysis of the "B" section, call the new tonic i. In other words, if your "A" section is in C major, call the C chords "I," and if your "B" section is in A minor, call the A minor chords "i." What you call the chords is always in relationship to the new key.**

- **Use your ears to tell you what's good, but don't forget to make use of the musical concepts that you've learned. Remember in the minor key that the seventh scale degree in the V and vii° chord is raised when the chord goes to I or VI.**

- **Enjoy yourself. This is an opportunity to put into practice all you have learned in a creative way. Enjoy the process and be proud of yourself!**

EXERCISE 12-A

Name: _____

Final Composition Project

A Section

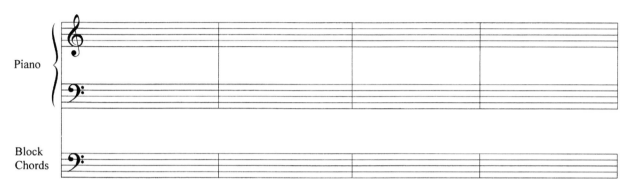

Piano

Block
Chords

Roman numeral
and inversions

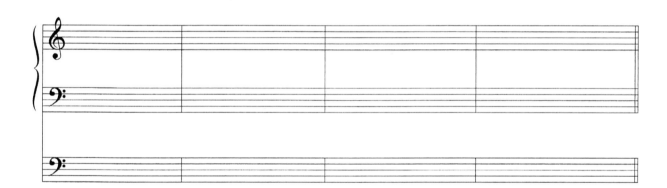

B Section

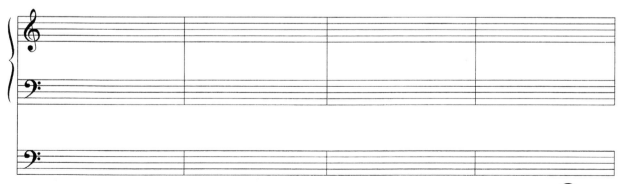

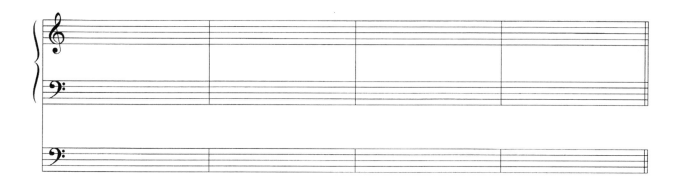

A Section

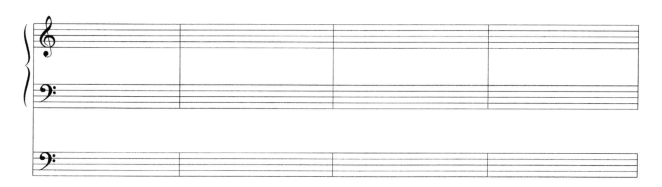

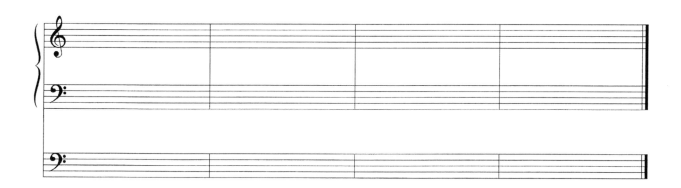

Index

pitch 1
pickup note (also anacrusis) 162
pickup measure 162
progressions 175–176
  in major keys 175
  in minor keys 176
  root motion by perfect fifth 176
pulse 21

R

relative major/minor key signatures 55
rests 25–26
rhythm 19–26, 35–36
  chart of values 20
  exercises in 35–39
root of chord
  defined 115
  finding 157–162

S

scale degrees named 42
scales 7, 41–42
  major 42–45
  minor 48–50
Scriabin, Alexander 27
Seventh chords 115, 120–122
  defined 115
  frequency of
    in major keys 138–139
    in minor keys 149
sharps, placement of 46
slurs 162, 183
staccato mark 162, 183
staff (plural "staves") 2
stems 19–20

T

tempo 27
tempo markings 27, 197
texture 115
  homophonic 115
  monophonic 115
  polyphonic 115
theme 98–99
time signature 21
tonality (tonal music) 41, 35–36
  defined 41
triads 115–124
  defined 115
  qualities 116–120
    augmented 117–120
    diminished 117, 120
    minor 116–117, 120
    major 116, 118, 120
triple meter 23
triplets 26–27
tuplets 26–27
  duplets 26
  quadruplets 26–27
  quintuplets 26–27
  triplets 26–27

U

upbeat 36

W

whole step 7